THE COMING
OF THE
SON OF MAN

THE SEQUENCE OF EVENTS
OF THE END TIMES

By
Janet M. Magiera

LWM Publications
Light of the Word Ministry

Versions quoted are noted by abbreviations after the verse citation as follows:

AMP: Amplified Bible, The Lockman Foundation, 2015.

APNT: Aramaic Peshitta New Testament Translation, LWM Publications, 2006.

ESV: English Standard Version, Crossway, a publishing ministry of Good News Publishers, 2001.

ISV: International Standard Version, Davidson Press, 1998.

KJV: King James Version of the English Bible, 1769 Blayney edition.

Lamsa: The Holy Bible from Ancient Eastern Manuscripts, A.J. Holman Company, 1968.

NASB: New American Standard Bible, The Lockman Foundation, 1977.

NET: The NET Bible, Biblical Studies Press, 1996.

NIV: New International Version, Biblica, Inc., 1973.

NLT: New Living Translation, Tyndale House Publishers, 1996.

Phillips: The New Testament in Modern English, 1958.

TNK: The Jewish Bible: Torah, Nevi'im, Kethuvim, Jewish Publication Society, 1985.

Copyright © 2019, Janet M. Magiera
ISBN 978-1-7326625-0-6

LWM Publications, Light of the Word Ministry
6213 Lake Athabaska Place
San Diego CA 92119
www.lightofword.org

FOREWORD

This is a book about the hope of Christ's return. As born-again children of God we have great anticipation for the gathering together to happen soon. We also have a great expectation of life in our new bodies.

Philippians 3:20-21
For our conversation is in heaven from whence we look for the Savior, the Lord Jesus Christ:
Who shall change our vile body that it may be fashioned like unto his glorious body, according to the working whereby he is able even to subdue all things unto himself.

Yet the gathering together is only the beginning of a series of profound prophecies in the Scriptures.

When we read of the events which occur with the opening of the seven seals recorded in the book of Revelation, the first thing that is obvious is that these will be trying times for the people going through them. Yet through all the events, we see the justice of God and His great heart of love for His people. His desire is that all men would be saved and He holds back judgment as long as possible. In the end He will put together the new heavens and new earth "wherein dwells righteousness."

The sequence of events of the end times is a difficult subject of study in God's Word. Many of the prophecies are not as clear as we would like, or do not give enough information to come to clear conclusions. A good thing to keep in mind is to handle difficult verses in light of the verses that are clear on a topic. Jan has done a masterful job of this.

This is by no means an exhaustive study of the subject, as that would require several volumes. However, she has handled each topic thoroughly, covering the salient verses on the subject. She clearly indicates what we can understand of the subject and points out the things we will only comprehend with the coming of Jesus Christ. Sometimes there is more than one way a scripture can be understood and some prophecies have dual fulfillments, both immediate and future. She points these out as well. Be sure to push through sections with a lot of detail to get the overall scope and then go back to study the details in more depth.

This book has added greatly to my understanding of the book of Revelation. It has also helped me to understand difficult sections of the books of Isaiah, Daniel, Ezekiel, Joel and others. It has also clarified much of the 24th chapter of Matthew for me.

The purpose of this book is for us to abound in hope. That means we can rejoice that God has it all figured out what the future will be. We can rest and have comfort in that assurance and be filled with joy and peace.

Romans 15:13
Now the God of hope fill you with all joy and peace in believing, that ye may abound in hope, through the power of the Holy Ghost.

I recommend this book to all those who love his appearing.

2 Timothy 4:8
Henceforth there is laid up for me a crown of righteousness, which the Lord, the righteous judge, shall give me at that day: and not to me only, but unto all them also that love his appearing.

Rev. Dan Connell
Aurora, Colorado

TABLE OF CONTENTS

INTRODUCTION

You are about to take a scriptural journey to the end of the age and learn how God defines the sequence and time frames of end time events. This book will take you through biblical prophecies and show what can be clearly understood. It will give you a firm foundation of hope in God's unfailing love in wanting everyone "to come to repentance." It will reveal the "glorious appearing of the great God and our Savior Jesus Christ" (Titus 2:13).

Life during these days on earth is certainly becoming darker and darker. Environmentalists are sounding alarms about the global warming of the atmosphere. New diseases, as well as old ones, are becoming more resistant to modern medicine. Economists are bewailing the multitrillion-dollar debts with no clear solutions to the problems. Earthquakes, storms and increasingly harsh weather are now commonplace. Wars and rumors of wars are heard around the world on a daily basis. No wonder there has been and continues to be rampant speculation about whether we are already in the tribulation described in the Old Testament! Is there any hope for the future? When will it all end? And can we know clear truth about the end times?

There definitely is hope concerning the future. The whole plan is revealed in the Word of God, the Bible. Not one prophecy recorded in the Bible has ever failed. All the prophecies regarding the birth of Christ were fulfilled, as well as proven prophecies regarding many nations of the world and wars which have already occurred. God's Word has stood the test of time, archaeology and history, confirming the truth in its pages. The Bible speaks of a hope that is not based on the ability of man to solve the complex problems of life in the 21st century.

INTRODUCTION

True hope is in the person of Jesus Christ—the Son of God, the Messiah—and his promised appearance to the Church of the Body now and to Israel in the future. Hope is a word that in its simplest verbal form means "to think, inspect or examine." It is the Hebrew verb *seber* and the Aramaic verb *sabar*. It is used in this simple form in Nehemiah 2:13, where Nehemiah went out and "inspected" the walls of Jerusalem. In the next intensive form, *seber* means "to wait for, hope for, or wait on."

Psalm 119:166 ESV
I hope [seber] for your salvation, O LORD, and I do your commandments.

The word in Hebrew for salvation here is *yeshuwah*, similar to Jesus' name, Yeshua, and means "deliverance or help." Hope expectantly considers that the promises of God will come to pass in his timing and with his insight. Hope is an aspect of faith: the expectant confidence that what God has promised, HE will bring to pass. In order to have this hope, we hold fast to this confidence.

Hebrews 3:6 APNT
Now Christ, as the Son, [is] over his house. And we are his house, if we hold fast the boldness and the boasting of his hope [savra] to the end.

There are many other verses about how hope in general provides a firm foundation on which we can base our lives. One crucial verse is in Hebrews.

Hebrew 6:17-19 APNT
Because of this, God especially wanted to show to the heirs of the promise that his promise would not change, so he bound it with oaths,

that by two things that are unchangeable in which God is not able to lie, we who have sought refuge in him may have great comfort and may hold fast to the hope that was promised to us, which we have as an anchor that holds our soul, so that it is not shaken...

Here again we see that we have to "hold fast" to the hope that was promised to us. Then that hope becomes like an anchor on a boat that holds our lives so that they are not disturbed, confused or shaken. This shaking is like what happens in an earthquake. There is sudden fear and abrupt confusion. But when a boat is anchored, there may be some rocking, but it remains firmly and steadily in place.

This is what will happen when we review the various keys in this book about how to understand the end times. With these keys, you will be able to calmly and straightforwardly know not only what to believe yourself, but also you will be able to discern with confidence what others say about the future. This kind of strength and confidence—not being moved—is vitally needed in this day and time.

In Ephesians 1:18, Paul's prayer for the faithful in Christ Jesus is that they "know what is the hope of his calling." The word "know" in Greek is *oida*, which means "to mentally perceive." An English derivative of this word is "video." Understanding the sequence of events of the end times will enable us to video or film the hope in a clearer way in our minds. We can stop or start the movie at any point and review it.

KEYS REGARDING "THE END OF THE AGE"

The second question we posed is, "When will it all end?" It depends on which "end" we are talking about.

9

INTRODUCTION

The answer lies in the difference between the words for "end." In Greek the words are *sunteleia* and *telos*. *Vine's Expository Dictionary of Old and New Testament Words* defines *sunteleia* as "a bringing to completion together, marking the completion or consummation of the various parts of a scheme.... The word does not denote a termination, but the heading up of events to the appointed climax."[1] E.W. Bullinger defines *telos* as "the fulfillment or completion of anything, i.e. its end or issue (not its cessation). It denotes strictly, not the ending of a departed state, but, the arrival of a complete or perfect one."[2] The Aramaic words also help us to understand the concepts, for there are two different words with separate roots. *Khartha* corresponds to *telos* and is from the root verb meaning "to be last." *Shulama* corresponds to *sunteleia* and comes from the root verb *shelem* which means "to complete or fulfill."

Putting these definitions together, the difference between the two words is easily understood in a time reference. The *sunteleia* includes all the events up until the final end point, *telos*, when the kingdom is delivered up to God. The *sunteleia* is the consummation or summary of events heading to a climax and *telos* is the last part of the completion of those events.

1 Corinthians 15:24 KJV
Then cometh the end [telos], when he shall have delivered up the kingdom to God, even the Father; when he shall have put down all rule and all authority and power.

---

[1] Vine, W.E., *Vine's Expository Dictionary of Old and New Testament Words*, p. 27.
[2] Bullinger, E.W. *A Critical Lexicon and Concordance to the English and Greek New Testament*, p. 248.

INTRODUCTION

The last enemy to be destroyed is death. This is the final event before the establishment of the new heavens and earth. It definitely denotes the arrival of a completed state. The final completion of God's judgments and plan of redemption ends when death is destroyed.

Each use of *sunteleia* and *telos* which refers to a specific event in the end times can now be understood.

Matthew 13:39b-40 APNT
...And the harvest is the culmination [sunteleia and shulama] of the age and the reapers [are] the angels.
As therefore the weeds are picked out and burned in the fire, so it will be in the culmination [sunteleia and shulama] of this age.

These two verses are from the parable of the tares of the field. When seeking to put this description in a particular place in the order of events, the point to understand first is that *sunteleia* could cover any event until the time death is destroyed. These verses must be studied in relation to other verses about the harvest, and about the time when the Devil and his demons are cast into the lake of fire.

Matthew 24:3 and 6 KJV
And as he sat upon the mount of Olives, the disciples came unto him privately, saying, Tell us, when shall these things be? and what shall be the sign of thy coming and of the end [sunteleia] of the world?
And ye shall hear of wars and rumours of wars: see that ye be not troubled: for all these things must come to pass, but the end [telos] is not yet.

> *Events in the sunteleia need to be understood in relation to other verses about the same topic*

11

INTRODUCTION

Jesus Christ describes some of the signs and events of the time right after the gathering together of the Church and his coming to the earth. In verse six when he says that "the end is not yet," it means that what he is describing is still only a portion of the events and is not the completion or fulfillment of all the events. Luke 21:9, which is the parallel record of Matthew 24, makes it clearer.

Luke 21:9 KJV
But when ye shall hear of wars and commotions, be not terrified: for these things must first come to pass; but the end [telos] is not by and by [immediately].

There is another word to understand from Matthew 24:3 about the end of the world. The word for "world" in Greek is *aion* and in Hebrew and Aramaic, *olam* and *alma* respectively. All these words are translated as "age, world or life" and when used with various prepositions, are "forever, eternal and everlasting." The range of the definitions has caused no end of confusion in theology. What is "forever and ever," for example?

The key to understanding the word "world" or "age" is to look at the root of the word in both Hebrew and Aramaic. The Hebrew verb *alam* means "to be hidden, concealed, secret."[3] *Olam* is derived from this verb and is used particularly in the sense of hidden time. It is used in the Old Testament most often with the preposition "to" and is usually translated "forever." Robert Beecham of Cheltenham, England, suggests we could paraphrase it as "as far as we can see" or "to the limit of our sight." He summarizes the various uses of *olam* (and correspondingly *aion*) with prepositions as follows:

- The phrase normally translated *for ever* (or *for the age*) means *to the limit of our sight* and is indefinite in duration.

---

[3] Harris, R. *Theological Wordbook of the Old Testament*, p. 671.

- The phrase translated *for ever and ever* (or *for ages of ages*) means *to the limit of our sight and beyond.*
- The phrase translated *from of old* (or *from the age*) means *from the limit of our sight (backwards).*
- The adjective αἰώνιος rather than *eternal, everlasting or age-lasting* means *outside the limit of our sight*, and must be translated in different ways according to its context.[4]

Applying this to the New Testament uses of *alma*, the phrase "forever and ever" or "to the age of the ages" would be understood as "as far as we can see and further." There is a portion of time that we can see now, but in the "age to come" there is part that we cannot see and that is still hidden. This gives us a simple way to understand all of the uses of *aion* in the New Testament.

The third question is, "Can we know clear truth about the end times?"

There are many books and teachings about the end times, some of which are very confusing and puzzling. Some teachers try to use prophecies from the Old Testament and the Gospels to point out the "signs of the times," and that things that are going on in the world right now are the end times. Some even have gone so far as to set a date when the Lord is returning based on astronomical data or current earthquakes and wars. How does one sort through all these things?

I believe that the Bible is clear about many of the events of the end times and that we CAN know what is revealed. There are certainly things that will be revealed in the future and will unfold as the events occur. But part of the reason for the book of Revelation is that many

---

[4] www.growthingod.org.uk/aion-and-olam.htm

events would be clarified. And further, there are blessings included in understanding these prophecies.

Revelation 1:1-3 APNT
The revelation of Jesus Christ that God gave to him to show to his servants what must happen soon. And he made [this] known when he sent by way of his angel to his servant John,
who gave witness to the word of God and to the witness of Jesus Christ, all that he saw.
Blessed [be] he who reads and those who hear the words of this prophecy and keep those [things] that are written in it, for the time has drawn near.

O⊤

The Gospels set the order of the events of the end times

The purpose of this book is to present the events of the end times in sequential order so that there is a framework to use to evaluate other verses, especially from the Prophets. There are three key sections which need to be examined together in order to see the full sequence of the end times. Because of their clarity in identifying the sequence of events, the four Gospels were used as the first step, making sure all the details fit within that framework. Then Revelation was studied to fit what was already known from the Gospels. The order of the seven seals meshed perfectly with the Gospel records. Then the Old Testament books of the Prophets were studied to give added understanding of the details.

Because this whole topic is concerning the future and thus is prophecy, there is much yet to be understood. But there is a definite order and symmetry which God has revealed that is possible to examine and understand. Once this pattern is seen, then all of the records concerning the end times fit together without contradiction.

CHAPTER 1 ⚓ BACKGROUND OF THE STUDY

An important concept to understand when studying this topic is the usage of words in the Bible for periods of time, specifically "day" and "times." A day can be a 24-hour period or it can represent a specific period of time which covers certain criteria. When the Bible says "day of ...." it is referring to a time period when that "something" is evident. This is especially important when endeavoring to understand the exact time frames of these specific phrases such as "the day of the Lord," "the day of judgment," "the day of God" and "the day of wrath." The specific "days" are noted in the various chapters and on the charts.

> **O—**
>
> *Day of... and times of... are key phrases to know when significant changes happen*

The word "times" is used to describe a block of time when significant changes happen. For example, Jesus referred to "the times of the Gentiles."

Luke 21:24 ESV
They will fall by the edge of the sword and be led captive among all nations, and Jerusalem will be trampled underfoot by the Gentiles, until the times of the Gentiles are fulfilled.

Also, in Peter's sermon after the man at the temple gate beautiful was healed in Acts 3, he spoke of "the times of restitution."

Acts 3:19-21 KJV
Repent ye therefore, and be converted, that your sins may be blotted out, when the times of refreshing shall come from the presence of the Lord;
And he shall send Jesus Christ, which before was preached unto you:

BACKGROUND OF THE STUDY

Whom the heaven must receive until the times of restitution of all things, which God hath spoken by the mouth of all his holy prophets since the world began.

When Jesus Christ comes back, there will be a restitution that brings a period of rest. This is the fulfillment of the rest, the *shabbat,* that was promised to the people of God.

Hebrews 4:8-10 ESV
For if Joshua had given them rest, God would not have spoken of another day later on.
So then, there remains a Sabbath rest for the people of God,
for whoever has entered God's rest has also rested from his works as God did from his.

When God had finished the six days of creation, Genesis says, "God did rest the seventh day from all his works." Then during the time of Joshua after the conquering of the Promised Land, the people had rest. But there is a future time that fulfills all the promises of "another day" and that is the 1,000-year reign of Christ on the earth. This will fulfill the Sabbath rest that has been promised to Israel.

But what is "the times of the Gentiles" referring to?

The book of Daniel contains the unfolding of what would happen to all the nations beginning with the Babylonian Empire. It was given as a vision in a dream to Nebuchadnezzar, which Daniel interpreted for him. The vision was of a statue made of various materials.

Daniel 2:31-35 ESV
"You saw, O king, and behold, a great image. This image, mighty and of exceeding brightness, stood before you, and its appearance was frightening.

BACKGROUND OF THE STUDY

The head of this image was of fine gold, its chest and arms of silver, its middle and thighs of bronze,
its legs of iron, its feet partly of iron and partly of clay.
As you looked, a stone was cut out by no human hand, and it struck the image on its feet of iron and clay, and broke them in pieces.
Then the iron, the clay, the bronze, the silver, and the gold, all together were broken in pieces, and became like the chaff of the summer threshing floors; and the wind carried them away, so that not a trace of them could be found. But the stone that struck the image became a great mountain and filled the whole earth.

Daniel told the king what the dream meant and what God had revealed to him.

Daniel 2:36-45 ESV
"This was the dream. Now we will tell the king its interpretation.
You, O king, the king of kings, to whom the God of heaven has given the kingdom, the power, and the might, and the glory,
and into whose hand he has given, wherever they dwell, the children of man, the beasts of the field, and the birds of the heavens, making you rule over them all– you are the head of gold.
Another kingdom inferior to you shall arise after you, and yet a third kingdom of bronze, which shall rule over all the earth.
And there shall be a fourth kingdom, strong as iron, because iron breaks to pieces and shatters all things. And like iron that crushes, it shall break and crush all these.
And as you saw the feet and toes, partly of potter's clay and partly of iron, it shall be a divided kingdom, but some of the firmness of iron shall be in it, just as you saw iron mixed with the soft clay.
And as the toes of the feet were partly iron and partly clay, so the kingdom shall be partly strong and partly brittle.

BACKGROUND OF THE STUDY

As you saw the iron mixed with soft clay, so they will mix with one another in marriage, but they will not hold together, just as iron does not mix with clay.
And in the days of those kings the God of heaven will set up a king-dom that shall never be destroyed, nor shall the kingdom be left to another people. It shall break in pieces all these kingdoms and bring them to an end, and it shall stand forever,
just as you saw that a stone was cut from a mountain by no human hand, and that it broke in pieces the iron, the bronze, the clay, the silver, and the gold. A great God has made known to the king what shall be after this. The dream is certain, and its interpretation sure."

This dream described the nations that would continue to rule over Jerusalem until God set up a "kingdom that will stand forever." The gold was the Babylonian Empire. The silver was the Medo-Persian Empire. The bronze was the Greek Empire under Alexander the Great. And the iron represented the Roman Empire, which split into two legs, east and west. The vision about the feet and toes was made clearer in a later vision to Daniel. In this later vision, the nations are represented by animals: a lion for Babylonia, a bear for Medo-Persia, a leopard for Greece, which did break apart into four parts (heads) after the death of Alexander the Great. The fourth beast was unique and had ten horns corresponding to the ten toes of the statue.[5]

Below is a rendering of what the statue might have looked like. Rev. Clarence Larkin was an American Baptist pastor, Bible teacher and author whose writings and charts had a great impact on conservative Protestant culture in the early 20th century.

---

[5] LaHaye, Tim. *Charting the End Times*, pp. 87-88.

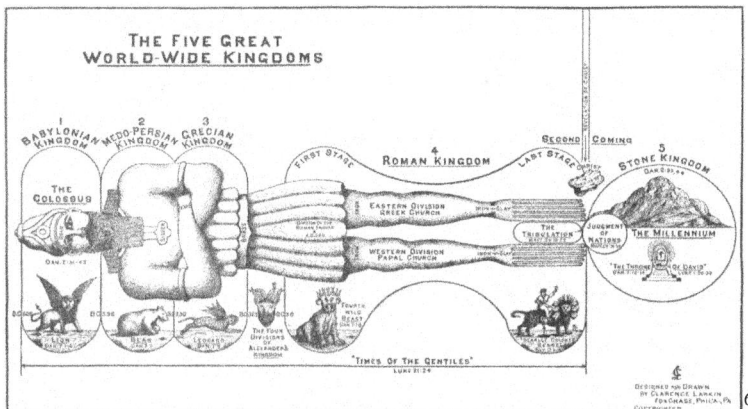

Daniel 7:7-8 ESV
After this I saw in the night visions, and behold, a fourth beast, ter-
rifying and dreadful and exceedingly strong. It had great iron
teeth; it devoured and broke in pieces and stamped what was left
with its feet. It was different from all the beasts that were before it,
and it had ten horns.
I considered the horns, and behold, there came up among them an-
other horn, a little one, before which three of the first horns were
plucked up by the roots. And behold, in this horn were eyes like the
eyes of a man, and a mouth speaking great things.

God sent an angel to explain the vision to Daniel.

Daniel 7:23-27 ESV
Thus he said: 'As for the fourth beast, there shall be a fourth king-
dom on earth, which shall be different from all the kingdoms, and
it shall devour the whole earth, and trample it down, and break it
to pieces.

---

[6] Larkin, Clarence. *The Book of Revelation*, p. 106.

As for the ten horns, out of this kingdom ten kings shall arise, and another shall arise after them; he shall be different from the former ones, and shall put down three kings.
He shall speak words against the Most High, and shall wear out the saints of the Most High, and shall think to change the times and the law; and they shall be given into his hand for a time, times, and half a time.
But the court shall sit in judgment, and his dominion shall be taken away, to be consumed and destroyed to the end.
And the kingdom and the dominion and the greatness of the kingdoms under the whole heaven shall be given to the people of the saints of the Most High; his kingdom shall be an everlasting kingdom, and all dominions shall serve and obey him.'

This fourth beast arises out of the remnants of the Roman Empire and will initially be an alliance of ten kings. Another king (a little horn) will rise out of this alliance and will take over three of the kingdoms. This is the description of the Antichrist who will then be destroyed by the coming of Jesus Christ.

Then also a new Jerusalem will be established, the times of the Gentiles will end and the times of restitution will begin. This is the overall scope of the end times.

Are you ready to begin the movie of the hope and to explore the sequence of events of the end times?

CHAPTER 2 ≑ THE GATHERING TOGETHER

The charts at the beginning of the chapters summarize the events that will be covered with pertinent verses listed next to the events.

Events	Scriptures
Coming of our Lord Dead in Christ rise first Alive in Christ are changed Meeting of our Lord in the air	1 Thessalonians 4:13-18
The last trump	1 Corinthians 15:51-57
Judgment seat (bema)	2 Corinthians 5:10 1 Corinthians 3:11-15
The great mystery complete	Ephesians 3:8-9
Day of Christ	Philippians 1:10; 2:16
Day of our Lord Jesus Christ	1 Corinthians 1:8; 5:5 2 Corinthians 1:14
Day of Redemption	Ephesians 4:30

The understanding of the gathering together of the Church of the Body of Christ is crucial to being able to distinguish the sequence of events of the end times. This "gathering together" is taken from a passage in 1 Thessalonians and specifically describes what will take place.

1 Thessalonians 4:15-17 APNT
Now this we say to you, by the word of our Lord, that we who remain at the coming of our Lord who are living will not overtake those who are asleep, because our Lord, with a command and with the voice of the archangel and with the trumpet of God, will come down from heaven and the dead who are in Christ will rise up first. And then we who remain who are living will be caught up with them as one in the clouds for the meeting of our Lord in the air and so we will always be with our Lord.

The word "caught up" is the Greek word *harpazo* which means to be seized or caught away. The Latin term is *rapturo*, from which the term "rapture" is derived. This catching away is definitely in terms of one place to another. The Aramaic word is *khetap*, which means to snatch out, carry up or off by force. I have chosen to refer to this event as the gathering together because that is the most familiar translation.

This time of the gathering together is called "the coming of our Lord." The word "coming" in Greek is *parousia* and in Aramaic it is *methitha*. Both words mean "arrival" or "coming" of a particular person at a particular time. A person could arrive at two similar locations, but if the details were different, then the times would not be the same. Such is the case with the various comings of Christ to the earth. There are some particular characteristics of the gathering together that illustrate three differences from other times the coming of the Lord is described.

> ⚊○
>
> *The coming (parousia) of Christ refers to several different times and locations*

The first difference is that this is a "meeting of our Lord in the air." All of the other descriptions of the future coming of Christ refer to his coming to the earth. There is no such meeting described or even hinted at in the Old Testament, the Gospels or the book of Revelation. Clearly, the gathering together cannot be the same event as the Lord returning "with ten thousands of his saints," because he then comes to the earth (Zechariah 14:4). Ezekiel 37:11-14 says that when the Old Testament believers are raised from the dead (at the resurrection of the just) they will go into the Promised Land. The Gospels also clearly say that Jesus Christ comes to the earth and conquers it, gathering the people from the four corners of the earth.

The second difference is what this "meeting" is all about. The Greek word is *apantesis*. This term was used in the first century culture to refer to meeting a king or important person a distance away from his desired place of arrival and then escorting that person to their destination. This happened to Paul when he was on his way to Rome and the believers went out to the Appii Forum to meet him. Their purpose was to then escort him to Rome.

Acts 28:15 APNT
And when the brothers who were there heard [of our coming], they went out to meet us [apantesis] as far as the square that was called Appii Forum and as far as the Three Taverns. And when Paul saw them, he gave thanks to God and was strengthened.

The Church of the Body of Christ will be meeting Christ in the air and then at some point will escort him back to the earth.

The third difference about this "coming" is that just as there was a distinct event that initiated the age of grace, the outpouring of the gift of the Holy Spirit on the day of Pentecost, so there must be a distinct event to close this age. A gathering of all Christians, living and dead, would qualify as such an event. This period of time between Pentecost and the gathering together is called a "mystery."

Ephesians 3:8-9 APNT
To me, who am the least of all the holy [ones], this grace was given, that I should declare among the Gentiles the wealth of Christ that is untraceable
and [that] I should bring light to everyone what is the administration of the mystery that was hidden from the ages in God, who created all [things],

The word "mystery" in Greek is *musterion* and in Aramaic *raza*. It means "a hidden purpose or counsel" and "is not obvious to the understanding."[7] The administration or "fellowship" (KJV) of the mystery was untraceable, meaning it was not found in the Old Testament scriptures; it was "hidden from the ages in God." As we saw in the introduction, "from the ages" could be understood as "from the limit of our sight backwards" or we could also paraphrase this, "as far back as we can see." In other words, God did not reveal what this time period was all about. In 1 Corinthians 2:8 (ESV) it says that "none of the rulers of this age understood this, for if they had, they would not have crucified the Lord of glory."

There are several different periods of time that God calls a mystery in the Church epistles. There is the mystery that "blindness in part is happened to Israel, until the fullness of the Gentiles be come in" (Romans 11:25). This refers to how it is not known today who the true Israel is. Only God knows the true lineage of the descendants of Israel. Another mystery is called "the mystery of iniquity" (2 Thessalonians 2:7). This will be explained in chapter 4. The majority of the references in the epistles have to do with the "mystery of Christ" (Ephesians 3:4).

Colossians defines what the mystery of Christ was and that it is now revealed.

Colossians 1:25-27 KJV
Whereof I am made a minister, according to the dispensation of God which is given to me for you, to fulfil the word of God;
Even the mystery which hath been hid from ages and from generations, but now is made manifest to his saints:
To whom God would make known what is the riches of the glory of this mystery among the Gentiles; which is Christ in you, the hope of glory:

---

[7] Thayer, Joseph Henry. *The New Thayer's Greek-English Lexicon*, p 420.

Christ is the central subject of the mystery. Prior to the revealing of the mystery, all of the blessings of God were given to the descendants of Abraham through Isaac and Jacob, who are called the Judeans or Jews. If Gentiles wanted to be a part of the covenant God made with the Judeans, they needed to first become proselytes and convert to Judaism. Even after the day of Pentecost when the first believers were born again, the outpouring of the gift of Holy Spirit was still primarily limited to Judeans or proselytes who believed that Jesus was the Messiah.

But then during the ministry of the apostle Paul, the "great mystery" (Ephesians 5:32) was revealed and not only included the Gentiles, but made them an integral part of a totally new entity called the "new man" in Ephesians.

Ephesians 2:13-18 APNT
But now, in Jesus Christ, you who previously were far have become near by the blood of Christ.
For he was our peace treaty, who made the two of them one and has broken down the wall that stood in the middle
and the conflict, by his flesh. And he brought to an end the law of commandments with its commandments, so that [from] the two of them he would create in himself one new man, and he made a peace treaty.
And he reconciled the two of them with God in one body and, by his cross, he destroyed the conflict.
And he came [and] he declared peace to you, [both] the far and the near,
because in him we both have access in one spirit to the Father.

What brought the Jews and Gentiles together was the access to the Father by the same Spirit. No longer was there a distinction between the two groups, but they became "one new man" (Ephesians 2:15). This is "the mystery of the gospel" that we preach (Ephesians 6:19).

25

THE GATHERING TOGETHER

Since this time period of the mystery began on the day of Pentecost, it must have an ending point, which is described as the gathering together. This ending point is also called "the day of Christ" and "the coming of our Lord."

THE DAY OF OUR LORD JESUS CHRIST

The description of the gathering together can be seen in the use of phrases with "day of...." The key phrases are "day of Christ," "day of our Lord Jesus Christ," and "day of redemption." In the first two references below from the Aramaic Peshitta New Testament, the phrase is specifically "day of our Lord Jesus Christ," rather than "day of the Lord Jesus" as in the Greek texts. This helps to distinguish that these uses are referring to the gathering together.

1 Corinthians 5:5 APNT
*and [that] you should deliver this [one] to Satan for the ruin of his body, so that he will live spiritually in the **day of our Lord Jesus Christ**.*

2 Corinthians 1:14 APNT
*as even you have acknowledged in part that we are your boasting, as also you are ours in the **day of our Lord Jesus Christ**.*

1 Corinthians 1:8 ESV
*...who will sustain you to the end, guiltless in the **day of our Lord Jesus Christ**.*

Philippians 1:10 NASB
*so that you may approve the things that are excellent, in order to be sincere and blameless until **the day of Christ**;*

Philippians 2:16 ESV
holding fast to the word of life, so that in **the day of Christ** *I may*
be proud that I did not run in vain or labor in vain.

Ephesians 4:30 APNT
And you should not grieve the sanctified Spirit of God, by whom
you were sealed until the **day of redemption**.

We are sealed with the gift of the Spirit until the day of redemption. The word "until" is the Greek word *eis*, meaning all the way toward a point. When something is sealed, it shows the sign of its authenticity. Seals were used in many cultures to guarantee that a letter or contract was genuine. We have been sealed with God's Spirit and it guarantees that we will receive our full inheritance.

Ephesians 1:13-14 APNT
In him also, you heard the word of truthfulness, which is the gospel
of your life, and in him, you believed and you were sealed with the
Holy Spirit that was promised,
which is the guarantee of our inheritance to the redemption of
those who have life and to the glory of his honor.

This sealing is a guarantee that we will have a full redemption from death to life and that we will also receive new bodies fashioned like Jesus' glorious resurrected body. The Hebrew word for "sealed" is *arabown* and it was used in the record of Judah giving his seal to Tamar as a pledge (Genesis 38:17-20). It was like a "credit card" and Judah exchanged it for a promise to take care of Tamar. God has given us a down payment (or use of his credit card) by the gift of the Spirit to continually remind us that the full redemption is coming in the future.

THE GATHERING TOGETHER

Romans 8:23 APNT
And they are not alone, but we also who have the first[fruit] of the
Spirit groan within ourselves and we wait for the adoption and the
redemption of our bodies,

Philippians 3:20-21 NET
But our citizenship is in heaven– and we also await a savior from
there, the Lord Jesus Christ,
who will transform these humble bodies of ours into the likeness of
his glorious body by means of that power by which he is able to
subject all things to himself.

What a glorious day that will be!

Now let's go back and look at the specific details of the gathering
together from 1 Thessalonians. Here the gathering together is called
"the coming of our Lord."

THE COMING OF OUR LORD

1 Thessalonians 4:15-17 APNT
Now this we say to you, by the word of our Lord, that we who re-
main at the coming of our Lord who are living will not overtake
those who are asleep,
because our Lord, with a command and with the voice of the arch-
angel and with the trumpet of God, will come down from heaven
and the dead who are in Christ will rise up first.
And then we who remain who are living will be caught up with
them as one in the clouds for the meeting of our Lord in the air
and so we will always be with our Lord.

The order of the events is:
1. A shout (command)
2. The voice of the archangel

3. The trumpet of God
4. The dead in Christ rise first
5. Those alive in Christ are changed
6. Both groups are caught up in the clouds
7. Meeting with our Lord in the air

First our Lord descends from heaven with a shout or a cry of command: "It's time!" Then the archangel chimes in his voice: "Get up!" and the trumpet of God sounds. The dead rise first and then those who are alive are changed and both groups are caught up (or gathered up) into the air for the meeting with our Lord.

The coming of our Lord is further explained in 1 Corinthians that this all happens in the twinkling of an eye.

1 Corinthians 15:51-57 APNT
Behold, I am telling you a mystery. Not all of us will sleep, but all of us will be changed,
suddenly, as the twinkling of an eye, at the last trumpet sounding, and the dead will rise without corruption and we will be changed. For this [one] that was going to be corrupted will put on incorruption. And this [one] that [was going to] die will put on immortality. Now when this [one] that is corrupted puts on incorruption, and this [one] that dies, immortality, then the saying will happen that is written: Death is swallowed in victory.
Where is your sting, death? Or where is your victory, grave? Now the sting of death is sin and the power of sin is the law. But blessed [be] God who gives us the victory by way of our Lord Jesus Christ.

There has been a lot of speculation about why the trumpet is called the "last trump." Thessalonians called it the trumpet of God so it cannot be the same as other trumpets in the book of Revelation which are blown by angels and are called *shofar*. This trumpet is blown in a very short moment of time, whereas the trumpets in Revelation sound over a number of days (Revelation 8-10).

The word "last" could be last in time or last in a sequence. The phrase here in Corinthians refers to a military use of the trumpet. First-century historian Josephus described the use of trumpet signals in the Roman army. The first trumpet signaled when the company was to take down the tents and get ready to shift camp. The second trumpet was to call them to line up. The last trumpet basically sounded, "March!" "Then do the trumpets give a sound a third time, that they are to go out."[8] It was time to shift camp!

The fact that Paul does not explain to the Corinthians, indicates that they commonly understood what he meant by the last trump. Being part of the Roman Empire, they were very familiar with the signals of "the last trump" used for Roman soldiers. It would have had a tremendous significance to them in light of those military uses of the day. The gathering together is preceded by this last trumpet signal, indicating that it is time to shift camp from the earth to forever be with our Lord.

This trumpet definitely is not the same as the trumpets (*shofar*) that were blown on the Day of Trumpets. If there is a comparison to the use of trumpets in the Old Testament, it comes from instructions in the book of Numbers and is regarding the movement of the camp.

The last trump is the signal to shift camp from the earth to forever be with the Lord

Numbers 10:2 ESV
Make two silver trumpets. Of hammered work you shall make them, and you shall use them for summoning the congregation and for breaking camp.

[8] Josephus, Flavius. *Wars of the Jews,* Book 3, Chapter 5, 4.

THE GATHERING TOGETHER

The events of the gathering together will all happen so quickly that there will in effect be no time between all of the events. Then death will be swallowed up in victory! We will have our redeemed bodies and be with the Lord Jesus Christ from that point on. The quotations in 1 Corinthians 15:54-55 are taken from two passages.

Isaiah 25:8a KJV
He will swallow up death in victory; and the Lord GOD will wipe away tears from off all faces...

Hosea 13:14 NIV
I will deliver this people from the power of the grave; I will redeem them from death. Where, O death, are your plagues? Where, O grave, is your destruction?

At the time of the gathering together, believers from the day of Pentecost until then will be ransomed from the power of the grave. Death will no longer be able to sting and the grave will no longer have any victory and TOGETHER we will be with the Lord forever.

THE BEMA

Once we are gathered together to meet the Lord in the air, then all the believers must stand before the judgment seat of Christ. This is referred to as the *bema*.

2 Corinthians 5:10 APNT
For all of us are going to stand before the judgment seat of Christ that each one may be rewarded [for] what was done by him in his body, whether of good or of evil.

A *bema* refers to a raised platform on which an official is seated when rendering judgment on certain legal cases or athletic events.

This judgment is regarding our works and is further explained in 1 Corinthians as what we have built on the foundation of Jesus Christ.

1 Corinthians 3:12-15 KJV
Now if any man build upon this foundation gold, silver, precious stones, wood, hay, stubble;
Every man's work shall be made manifest: for the day shall declare it, because it shall be revealed by fire; and the fire shall try every man's work of what sort it is.
If any man's work abide which he hath built thereupon, he shall receive a reward.
If any man's work shall be burned, he shall suffer loss: but he himself shall be saved; yet so as by fire.

Our good works will be rewarded and the bad will be burned up. The rewards are given for our service.

Colossians 3:24 APNT
And know that from our Lord you will receive a reward in the inheritance, for you serve the LORD the Messiah.

If that was all we knew about the end times, it would be amazing! But that is not all there is, so let's explore what happens after the mass exodus of billions of people after the gathering together.

CHAPTER 3 ⚊ THE BEGINNING OF SORROWS

Events	Scriptures
False messiahs, propaganda campaign	Matthew 24:4-8
Wars and rumors of wars	Mark 13:5-8
Famine	Luke 21:8-11a
Death from earthquakes, pestilence, natural disasters and wild beasts	
1st four seals	Revelation 6:1-8
¼ of the population of the earth is killed	
One generation	Luke 21:29-33

An event called "the beginning of sorrows" happens right after the gathering together. In Matthew 24:8, Jesus Christ labeled it with this title when he discussed the signs of the *sunteleia* with his disciples. It covers the time immediately following the gathering together of the Church of the Body until the great tribulation, including the initial events of that time and then the rise of the Antichrist.

From the time when billions of people exit the earth in the gathering together, there is mass confusion and life is immediately changed. This time period can best be pictured by understanding the word "sorrows." Sorrow means "a throe, a pain, a pang, especially of a woman in travail."[9] This period right after the gathering together is like the beginning of labor for a woman having a child. There are definite signals that the birth is coming, but often contractions are sporadic and mild. Then eventually the contractions, usually with the breaking of waters, develop in intensity and the spacing of the contractions becomes regular. As the second or transition stage of labor approaches, the intensity continues to build. The great tribulation will be comparable to this very intense part of labor.

---

[9] Bullinger, E.W. *Figures of Speech Used in the Bible*, p. 991.

Hosea 13:12-13a KJV
The iniquity of Ephraim is bound up; his sin is hid.
The sorrow of a travailing woman shall come upon him...

A man does not actually experience labor, but during this time period, he will also personally identify with it.

Jeremiah 30:6 ESV
Ask now, and see, can a man bear a child? Why then do I see every man with his hands on his stomach like a woman in labor? Why has every face turned pale?

THE SEALS OF REVELATION

John has a vision of God's throne in heaven and all the participants around the throne (Revelation 4). Then Revelation 5 describes a scroll sealed with seven seals.

Revelation 5:1 NET
Then I saw in the right hand of the one who was seated on the throne a scroll written on the front and back and sealed with seven seals.

The scroll was written on the front and the back and probably sealed in seven different places as it was rolled up. Roman law required that people sealed their wills seven times because they were very important documents. Seven is a perfect number and also suggested the nature of the revelation it contained was extremely important. "In John's day, people used a seal to keep the contents of a document secret, unchangeable and free from tampering until some authoritative person broke the seal."[10]

---

[10] Constable, Thomas L. *Notes on Revelation,*
https://www.studylight.org/commentaries/dcc/revelation-5.html.

THE BEGINNING OF SORROWS

Revelation 5:2-5 ESV
And I saw a mighty angel proclaiming with a loud voice, "Who is
worthy to open the scroll and break its seals?"
And no one in heaven or on earth or under the earth was able to
open the scroll or to look into it,
and I began to weep loudly because no one was found worthy to
open the scroll or to look into it.
And one of the elders said to me, "Weep no more; behold, the Lion
of the tribe of Judah, the Root of David, has conquered, so that he
can open the scroll and its seven seals."

This Lion of the tribe of Judah is none other than Jesus Christ and is
also described as the Lamb. He is the only one who has the authority
to break the seals. The prophecies that follow in Revelation 6-22 are
the unfolding of what the scroll contains as each seal is opened. This
scroll may also be part of the "words" and "book" that Daniel was
instructed to seal until the time of the end.

Daniel 12:4 ESV
But you, Daniel, shut up the words and seal the book, until the time
of the end. Many shall run to and fro, and knowledge shall in-
crease.

THE FIRST FOUR SEALS

Jesus Christ describes the events of the beginning of sorrows in the
Gospels. His description is the key to understanding the first four
seals described in Revelation 6:1-8 that the Lamb opens. First there
will be false christs (messiahs) and many will be deceived.

Matthew 24:5 KJV
For many shall come in my name, saying, I am Christ; and shall
deceive many.

Luke 21:8 NET
He said, "Watch out that you are not misled. For many will come
in my name, saying, 'I am he,' and, 'The time is near.' Do not fol-
low them!

This corresponds to the false messiah on the white horse in Revelation 6:2 which John sees after the first seal is broken.

Revelation 6:2 KJV
And I saw, and behold a white horse: and he that sat on him had a
bow; and a crown was given unto him: and he went forth conquer-
ing, and to conquer.

The picture is a counterfeit of the true Christ coming on a white
horse as described in Revelation 19:11-16. There will be people who
will come in the name of Christ and they will conquer many.

This first horseman has been a source of dispute with some teachers.
Some have said it has to be Jesus Christ because of his riding a white
horse, but Jesus does not come back until much later after the tribulation is complete. This is just the "beginning." Others have indicated that this must be the Antichrist since he is imitating the true
Messiah. However, the Antichrist has yet to be revealed at this point.

The key to understanding this horseman is in the word for "bow."
In Aramaic, it is an archery bow, *qeshta*, and comes from a verb in
Aramaic that means "to shoot straight as an arrow." The Hebrew
word for bow is *qeshet* and is used regarding words and lies in a
number of places in the Scriptures. Here are two:

Jeremiah 6:23 NASB
"They seize bow and spear; They are cruel and have no mercy;
Their voice roars like the sea, And they ride on horses, Arrayed as
a man for the battle Against you, O daughter of Zion!"

THE BEGINNING OF SORROWS

Jeremiah 9:3 ESV
They bend their tongue like a bow; falsehood and not truth has
grown strong in the land; for they proceed from evil to evil, and
they do not know me, declares the LORD.

I believe that the very first thing that happens in the beginning of sorrows is that there is a giant propaganda campaign, with lies sent out like arrows in a bow in an attempt to explain the cataclysm that has just happened with the gathering together. The removal of that many people at one time certainly would need to be explained. The lies have to do with "false messiahs" and set the stage for the emergence and rise of the Antichrist.

Before any major war, there has been a concerted effort to win people over to one side or the other. Consider the conquering of the German people under Hitler in the years before World War II through propaganda. It is not surprising to discover that this first white horseman conquers with words, not actual arrows. Richard Ritenbaugh, of Forerunner Magazine's "Prophecy Watch," sums up the description of the bow that it "suggests a counterfeit 'truth' or a false gospel...the white horse and its rider represent religious deception."[11]

The second event Jesus describes is about wars and rumors of wars.

Mark 13:7-8a KJV
And when ye shall hear of wars and rumours of wars, be ye not
troubled: for such things must needs be; but the end shall not be
yet.
For nation shall rise against nation, and kingdom against king-
dom....

---

[11] www.cgg.org: "The Four Horsemen (Part Two) The White Horse, May 2004.

This phrase about nations rising against nations is to be understood as a Jewish idiom which means that there is a total conflict of the area, in this case, the whole world.[12]

This corresponds to the opening of the second seal, revealing one on a red horse:

Revelation 6:4 KJV
And there went out another horse that was red: and power was given to him that sat thereon to take peace from the earth, and that they should kill one another: and there was given unto him a great sword.

The order of the next two events varies in the Gospels. Matthew 24:7 has "famines, pestilences and earthquakes," Mark 13:8 says, "earthquakes, famines and troubles," and Luke 21:11 says, "earthquakes, famines, pestilences, fearful sights." This is not hard to understand when the third and fourth seals are studied. The third seal is famine and the fourth is death.

Revelation 6:5-8 APNT
And when the third seal was opened, I heard the third living creature, saying, "Come." And behold, [there was] a black horse and he who sat on it had a balance in his hand.
And I heard a voice from among the living creatures, saying, "A measure of wheat for a denarius and three measures of barley for a denarius and do not hurt the wine and the oil."
And when he opened the fourth seal, I heard the voice of the living creature, saying, "Come."
And I saw a pale horse and the name of him who sat on it [was] Death and Sheol followed him. And authority was given to him

---

[12] Fuchtenbaum, Arnold, *The Footsteps of the Messiah*, p. 63-64.

over one-fourth of the earth to kill by the sword and by famine and by death and by the wild animal[s] of the earth.

The opening of the third seal, revealing a black horse representing famine, includes all disasters which cause famine. Earthquakes may cause famines. A penny or denarius is one day's wage for the common person. It will take a whole day's work to earn a loaf of bread. There will be no money left over for anything else! "Hurt not the oil and wine" has to do with those who are wealthy who will control the famine.[13]

The opening of the fourth seal reveals death on a pale horse and hell following. The disasters listed in the Gospels all bring death: earthquakes, pestilence, trouble, fearful sights. The word "death" in Revelation and "pestilence" in the Gospels are tied together in the Aramaic. The word for pestilence in Matthew 24:7 is *mautana* and it literally means a "way of dying" and can be translated as plague, pestilence, mortality or slaughter. Its root verb is "to die."[14] The fourth part of the earth is killed in these first four seals. Hell means the grave and that is why it is following the fourth horse. It is no wonder that when the Antichrist rises up as a powerful king and ushers in peace, safety and prosperity, people embrace him with welcome arms!

ONE GENERATION

There is an important key to remember when we hear different teachings that we are "living in the end times." Even though there has been an escalation of wars, earthquakes and other natural disasters in the last hundred years, there has never been a time when one fourth of the population of the earth has been killed in a very short period of time. This is an unprecedented amount of people and is

---

[13] Bullinger, E.W. *Commentary on Revelation*, p. 257.
[14] Smith, J. Payne. *A Compendious Syriac Dictionary*, p. 260.

only the "beginning of sorrows." That would amount, in today's terms, to about one and a half billion people even after approximately two billion Christians are gone!

The first four seals happen in one generation when ¼ of the population of the earth is killed

After the description of the beginning of sorrows in the Gospels, Jesus then tells a parable and compares looking at a fig tree to knowing when all these things will come to pass.

Luke 21:29-33 ESV
And he told them a parable: "Look at the fig tree, and all the trees. As soon as they come out in leaf, you see for yourselves and know that the summer is already near.
So also, when you see these things taking place, you know that the kingdom of God is near.
Truly, I say to you, this generation will not pass away until all has taken place.
Heaven and earth will pass away, but my words will not pass away.

The phrase about "this generation" has also caused no end of confusion and conflict about why Jesus' coming did not happen right away in the first century. The answer is that the time period of the mystery was hid in God and not revealed until after the day of Pentecost. Once the gathering together happens, then there will be less than a generation (around 50 years) before Jesus Christ will come back as King of kings and Lord of lords.

The description of the first four seals elicits images of oncoming and terrifying events causing destruction and death. If this is just the beginning, what happens next? Is your interest piqued in the movie so far?

CHAPTER 4 ⚕ RISE OF THE ANTICHRIST

Events	Scriptures
"Man of sin"	2 Thessalonians 2:3
"Little horn"	Daniel 7:7-8
Rise of powerful "king"	Daniel 7:23-26
	Daniel 8:23-25
"Vile person"	Daniel 11:21-44
"Beast"	Revelation 13:1-18
Makes covenant with Israel for seven years Temple rebuilt and offerings reinstated	Daniel 9:24-27
Reign of "harlot"	Revelation 17:1-7
	Revelation 17:14-18
False death and resurrection	Revelation 17:8-13

The Antichrist comes into power after a succession of kings. It is very interesting how he comes into power and exactly what his place is in history. This place in history is foretold in Daniel's explanation of Nebuchadnezzar's dream in Daniel 2:31-45. It is important to read this section again at this time to get an understanding of the times of the end. The Antichrist will come from a specific time which is still future, but it is in the time period of the "ten toes" described in Daniel and the resurrection of the Roman Empire.

Another point to keep in mind is that the Devil does not know when Christ will return to gather the present church. In 2 Thessalonians 2:7, it is explained that the "mystery of wickedness has already begun to work, however, [it will work] by itself when that which now holds [it] back is taken away from the middle (APNT)." The NIV translation calls it "the secret power of lawlessness." In every generation since the time of the Roman Empire, the Devil had to have all in place so that if the Church of the Body was "taken out of the middle," he could quickly put all in motion for the takeover of the world ruler known as the Antichrist. That is why it seems that there have been attempts along this line throughout the last 2,000 years, for example, Napoleon, Hitler, Stalin, etc. But those attempts were only the mystery of lawlessness or iniquity at work. The actual rise of the Antichrist of the book of Revelation will not happen until the restraining power of the Holy Spirit in each Christian is taken away. Knowing this and the history of Daniel will prevent the biblical student from assuming that these prophesies are occurring in the present time.

The Antichrist is definitely a man as 2 Thessalonians 2:3 calls him "that man of sin" and the "son of perdition." His various titles or names show his main characteristics and how he rises to great power and influence over the whole world.

The vision Daniel had of the four great beasts reveals how the Antichrist will rise out of a group of ten kingdoms.

THE CHARACTERISTICS OF THE ANTICHRIST

Daniel 7:7-8 NET
"After these things, as I was watching in the night visions a fourth beast appeared– one dreadful, terrible, and very strong. It had two large rows of iron teeth. It devoured and crushed, and anything that was left it trampled with its feet. It was different from all the beasts that came before it, and it had ten horns.
As I was contemplating the horns, another horn– a small one– came up between them, and three of the former horns were torn out by the roots to make room for it. This horn had eyes resembling human eyes and a mouth speaking arrogant things.

One of the Antichrist's titles is the "little horn" as in the above verse. Horns of animals have always functioned for them as both offensive and defensive weapons. "By metonymy, horn came to symbolize those who had power: political or military…the horns represent both the foreign powers themselves and the condition of their strength and influence."[15]

When the angel explained the vision to Daniel, he told him that the horns were ten kingdoms.

Daniel 7:23-26 NET
This is what he told me: The fourth beast means that there will be a fourth kingdom on earth that will differ from all the other kingdoms. It will devour all the earth and will trample and crush it.
The ten horns mean that ten kings will arise from that kingdom. Another king will arise after them, but he will be different from the earlier ones. He will humiliate three kings.
He will speak words against the Most High. He will harass the holy ones of the Most High continually. His intention will be to change times established by law. They will be delivered into his hand For a time, times, and half a time.
But the court will convene, and his ruling authority will be removed– destroyed and abolished forever!

In other visions given to Daniel, that man is described further as a "king of fierce countenance" (KJV).

Daniel 8:23-24 NASB
And in the latter period of their rule, When the transgressors have run their course, A king will arise, Insolent and skilled in intrigue. And his power will be mighty, but not by his own power, And he will destroy to an extraordinary degree And prosper and perform his will; He will destroy mighty men and the holy people.

The Antichrist comes in with peace and prosperity. The sorrows of the beginning (wars, famines, pestilence) are basically stopped and

---

[15] Ryken, Leland, ed. *Dictionary of Biblical Imagery*, p. 400.

he works deceitfully to obtain the kingdom. His deceitfulness is prominent because he uses peace and prosperity to convince the people that he is great.

Daniel 8:25 KJV
And through his policy also he shall cause craft to prosper in his hand; and he shall magnify himself in his heart, and by peace shall destroy many: he shall also stand up against the Prince of princes; but he shall be broken without hand.

Some other titles revealed to Daniel are "the prince that shall come" (Daniel 9:26) and "a vile person" (Daniel 11:21). From these titles it is indicated that he is powerful, wicked and totally against the true God.

Finally, in the book of Revelation, he is called "the beast" in most translations.

Revelation 13:1 APNT
And I stood on the sand of the sea. And I saw a creature coming up from the sea that had ten horns and seven heads, and on his horns, ten crown headbands, and on his head, the name of blasphemy.

There is a variant reading in some Aramaic manuscripts for "creature" or "beast" as "savage beast," literally, a "beast of tooth," used throughout Revelation to distinguish this beast from the four living creatures around the throne. Jennings' *Syriac New Testament Lexicon* documents that the Lee manuscript uses this phrase 33 times.[16] Do the ten horns sound familiar from the description in Daniel? The Antichrist rises out of the ten kingdoms of the "toes" of Daniel 2.

---

[16] Jennings, William. *Lexicon to the Syriac New Testament*, p. 227.

A beast is used in the Scriptures to represent a Gentile government or kingdom and a horn is symbolic of leaders of a state, either civil or religious.

The beast in the book of Revelation is the Antichrist. His main characteristic, which is repeated in various passages, is that he does as he pleases and speaks against God. This is subtle at first, but as the tribulation opens, he will wage full-scale war with the saints.

Daniel 11:35 NLT
The king will do as he pleases, exalting himself and claiming to be greater than every god, even blaspheming the God of gods. He will succeed, but only until the time of wrath is completed. For what has been determined will surely take place.

From Daniel 11, we learn that the Antichrist rises up swiftly by using deceit and intrigue and destroys three of the ten kings in his rise to power. Reading on in chapter 11, verses 37-44, we also learn:

1. He will show no regard for the religion of his ancestors
2. He will have "no regard for the desire of women." He will either be asexual or homosexual.
3. He will not believe in any god at all (except for himself).
4. He will claim to be greater than any god.
5. He will only honor a "god" of the military. His whole focus and attention will be on his military forces.
6. He will conquer lands and distribute them.

It is clear from five passages in the Old Testament that the Antichrist will be an Assyrian. There has been much speculation if he will be Islamic or not. What we know from the Bible is that when the Messiah comes, he will deliver Israel and bring them peace. I have included this section so that we remember clearly that the Antichrist will be completely defeated and will only be allowed to rule for a very short time.

Micah 5:5-6 NASB
And this One will be our peace. When the Assyrian invades our land, When he tramples on our citadels, Then we will raise against him Seven shepherds and eight leaders of men.
And they will shepherd the land of Assyria with the sword, The land of Nimrod at its entrances; And He will deliver us from the Assyrian When he attacks our land And when he tramples our territory.

Assyria captured the northern tribes and Israel and took them into captivity. This prophecy's complete fulfillment is still future.

Isaiah 10:24-27 NASB
Therefore thus says the Lord God of hosts, "O My people who dwell in Zion, do not fear the Assyrian who strikes you with the rod and lifts up his staff against you, the way Egypt did.
For in a very little while My indignation against you will be spent, and My anger will be directed to their destruction."
And the LORD of hosts will arouse a scourge against him like the slaughter of Midian at the rock of Oreb; and His staff will be over the sea, and He will lift it up the way He did in Egypt.
So it will be in that day, that his burden will be removed from your shoulders and his yoke from your neck, and the yoke will be broken because of fatness.

These verses corroborate that the Assyrian will be soundly defeated.

Isaiah 14:24-25 ESV
The LORD of hosts has sworn: "As I have planned, so shall it be, and as I have purposed, so shall it stand,

that I will break the Assyrian in my land, and on my mountains tram-
ple him underfoot; and his yoke shall depart from them, and his bur-
den from their shoulder."

Isaiah 30:31 KJV
For through the voice of the LORD shall the Assyrian be beaten
down, which smote with a rod.

Isaiah 31:8 KJV
Then shall the Assyrian fall with the sword, not of a mighty man;
and the sword, not of a mean man, shall devour him: but he shall
flee from the sword, and his young men shall be discomfited.

HOW THE ANTICHRIST COMES TO POWER

Daniel 11:3-4 has a description of the rise of four rulers after Alexander the Great. The kingdom was divided under Alexander's four
generals. The two which became the strongest are called the king of
the south and the king of the north. This was fulfilled in the dynasty
of the Ptolemies in Egypt and the Seleucids in Syria. Daniel 11:5-
20 is a detailed description of exactly what happened between Egypt
and Syria (or Assyria) over a period of 135 years. Whichever king
was the strongest controlled the land of Israel also. For more details,
please refer to John Walvoord's *Commentary on Daniel.*

In Daniel 11:21-36, the prophecy begins to have fulfillment in the
person of Antiochus IV, who was a descendant of the Seleucids,
kings of the north. It is also an example of a multiple or partial fulfillment of a prophecy. As this ruler rose up in power, his name was
changed to Antiochus Epiphanes, which means, "the illustrious." He
came to power in the same way as the Antichrist during the end
times will. He is called a "vile person."

Daniel 11:21-23 KJV
And in his estate shall stand up a vile person, to whom they shall
not give the honour of the kingdom: but he shall come in peacea-
bly, and obtain the kingdom by flatteries.
And with the arms of a flood shall they be overflown from before
him, and shall be broken; yea, also the prince of the covenant.
And after the league made with him he shall work deceitfully: for
he shall come up, and shall become strong with a small people.

He is not supposed to be in the succession, but obtains the kingdom
by killing his rivals and using bribes and flatteries. Once he is in
power, he turns on the people of Israel with a great persecution.

Daniel 11:24-28 ESV
Without warning he shall come into the richest parts of the prov-
ince, and he shall do what neither his fathers nor his fathers' fa-
thers have done, scattering among them plunder, spoil, and goods.
He shall devise plans against strongholds, but only for a time.
And he shall stir up his power and his heart against the king of the
south with a great army. And the king of the south shall wage war
with an exceedingly great and mighty army, but he shall not stand,
for plots shall be devised against him.
Even those who eat his food shall break him. His army shall be
swept away, and many shall fall down slain.
And as for the two kings, their hearts shall be bent on doing evil.
They shall speak lies at the same table, but to no avail, for the end
is yet to be at the time appointed.
And he shall return to his land with great wealth, but his heart
shall be set against the holy covenant. And he shall work his will
and return to his own land.

Antiochus' career is also described in 1 and 2 Maccabees, the apoc-
ryphal books about the wars and the changes in the priesthood. One
of the things he did in the persecution against the Jewish people is

that he set up an image of Zeus at the temple altar. He demanded sacrifice to this image and later desecrated the temple by sacrificing a pig on it. This is how we know that there must be multiple fulfillments of this prophecy because in the future the Antichrist will actually set up an image of HIMSELF in the temple and call himself God, demanding worship of himself directly. Even though Antiochus assumed the title "Theos" on his coins, as Walvoord describes, "The identification of this passage with Antiochus, however, breaks down as the prophecy unfolds. For example, rather than magnifying himself 'above every god,' Antiochus tried to force the Jews to worship the typical Hellenistic pantheon of gods."[17] The next chapter will explain more of the details of the "abomination of desolation."

Daniel 11:35 is the verse which turns a corner, and from this verse on, the prophecy is about things which have not been fulfilled yet. The reason we know this is that "the time of the end" and "the time of wrath" is still future.

> **O—**
> *Prophecy can have partial or multiple fulfillments*

Daniel 11:35-36 NLT
And some of the wise will fall victim to persecution. In this way, they will be refined and cleansed and made pure until the time of the end, for the appointed time is still to come.
The king will do as he pleases, exalting himself and claiming to be greater than every god, even blaspheming the God of gods. He will succeed, but only until the time of wrath is completed. For what has been determined will surely take place.

It is apparent from this brief overview of Daniel 11 that there will be parallel fulfillments when the Antichrist rises to power including similar characteristics as described earlier.

---

[17] Walvoord, John. *Daniel*, p. 350.

Early in his rise to power, the Antichrist makes a covenant or league with many people (Daniel 9:27a, 11:23). It does not state in Daniel or Revelation exactly with whom this covenant is made or what its purpose is. It appears to be the league which stops all the wars, but most likely it is a league with the religious powers centered in Jerusalem and involves the establishment of a Jewish temple in Jerusalem. In any case, this "new covenant" brings great peace and prosperity.

How the Antichrist becomes a world leader is further explained in Revelation 13. His power is given him by the Dragon.

Revelation 13:2 KJV
And the beast which I saw was like unto a leopard, and his feet were as the feet of a bear, and his mouth as the mouth of a lion: and the dragon gave him his power, and his seat, and great authority.

Beast from the Sea - Clarence Larkin[18]

Revelation 13:1-18 describes the Antichrist's rise to power in detail and what he does. His actions are orchestrated to be like the true Christ in every way possible. In fact, initially he makes himself look like the Messiah so many people will follow him and believe. The world will believe that he is the returned Christ. The prefix "anti"

---

[18] Larkin, Clarence. *The Book of Revelation*, p. 119.

does not mean that he will be simply against Christ. It also signifies that this man will rule "in the place of" Christ.

The Antichrist deceives people when he receives a deadly wound and this wound is healed (Revelation 13:3). The Dragon (Satan) makes it look as though he has died and been raised from the dead. Revelation 17:8-13 describes him as "the beast that was, and is not, and yet is." That is how he can be both the seventh and eighth king (note that the number eight signifies his new beginning). Then the false prophet (a powerful religious figure styled like Elijah), also called a beast, rises up to cause the earth to worship "the beast whose wound was healed." He does great signs and wonders and deceives the people.

Revelation 13:12-14 KJV:
And he exerciseth all the power of the first beast before him, and causeth the earth and them which dwell therein to worship the first beast, whose deadly wound was healed.
And he doeth great wonders, so that he maketh fire come down from heaven on the earth in the sight of men,
And deceiveth them that dwell on the earth by the means of those miracles which he had power to do in the sight of the beast; saying to them that dwell on the earth, that they should make an image to the beast, which had the wound by a sword, and did live.

This triad or "trinity" of power of the Dragon, the beast and the false prophet will manipulate their credentials so that it looks like the kingdom of God that was prophesied has occurred on earth.[19] Then the Antichrist will destroy the worldwide religion and tolerate no other worship except for himself.

---

[19] Martin, Ernest. *The Life and Times of the Antichrist,* pp. 50-51.

REIGN OF THE HARLOT

There is an interesting description of the whore called Mystery Babylon in Revelation 17. She is described as riding the same beast as the description of the Antichrist. She is a key player in the Antichrist's rise to power.

Revelation 17:3-6 APNT
And he led me to the wilderness spiritually and I saw a woman
who was sitting on the red creature that was full of the names of
blasphemy that had seven heads and ten horns.
And the woman was clothed with purple and scarlet [garments]
that were gilded with gold and precious stones and pearls and she
had a cup of gold in her hand and it was full of the abomination
and pollution of her fornication.
And on her forehead it was written, "Mystery, Babylon the great,
mother of harlots and of pollutions of the earth."
And I saw that the woman was drunk from the blood of the holy
[ones] and from the blood of the witnesses of Jesus. And I won-
dered [with] great wonder when I saw her.

The vision of the woman riding the beast indicates that she is supported by the political power of the beast and on the other hand that she is in a dominant role at least during this rise of the Antichrist. She is called Babylon because Satan's false religious systems all originated in Babylon with Nimrod, the great grandson of Ham and his wife Semiramis. In Genesis 10:9 he is called "a mighty hunter." The Targum of Jonathan (an ancient Jewish commentary) interprets this to mean "a mighty rebel before the Lord."[20] Nimrod's purpose and the purpose of every idolatrous religion since was to draw people away from the worship of the one true God.

---

[20] Bullinger, E.W. *Commentary on Revelation*, p. 507.

A harlot is used as a symbol of a false religion or church

Revelation 17:7-18 interprets the vision and explains that the woman prostitute has seduced many nations and peoples. But also, this section clarifies that the kingdom of the beast will not allow the religious system to continue to be powerful once he comes into power.

Revelation 17:15-16 APNT
And he said to me, "The waters that you saw, on which the harlot sits, are nations and multitudes and peoples and languages.
And the ten horns that you saw of the creature will hate the harlot and they will make her desolate and naked and they will eat her flesh and they will burn her with fire.

Many people through the centuries have interpreted the whore as Papal Rome. Certainly, there are characteristics that Catholicism incorporated which were originally parts of other pagan rituals, but this woman pictured in Revelation will be a worldwide ecumenical movement that will be supported by many different religions. Since this is a vision, it is important not to read too much into the details. All will become clear as the end times unfold. What we do know is that the religion represented by the city Babylon will be destroyed very quickly.

Revelation 18:21 NET
Then one powerful angel picked up a stone like a huge millstone, threw it into the sea, and said, "With this kind of sudden violent force Babylon the great city will be thrown down and it will never be found again!

After the Antichrist is in full power, he will break the covenant and begin to gather armies to besiege Jerusalem. This begins the great tribulation which is described in the next chapter. Now it is important to understand the timing of all of these events.

DANIEL'S 70 WEEKS

In Daniel 9, the prophet was reading in the book of Jeremiah about how there would be 70 years of captivity under Babylon. Since that time was going to be shortly completed at this point in Daniel's life, he began to intercede for his beloved people very earnestly.

Daniel 9:20-23 Lamsa
And while I was yet praying and confessing my offenses and the offenses of my people Israel and presenting my supplication before the LORD my God for the holy mountain of my God,
Yea, while I was speaking in prayer, the man Gabriel, whom I had seen in the vision before, came from heaven, flying swiftly, and drew near me at the time of the evening sacrifice.
And he came and talked to me and said to me, O Daniel, I am now come forth to instruct you, so that you might understand.
At the beginning of your prayer, the word came forth and I have come to make it known to you; for you are greatly beloved; therefore discern the matter and understand the vision.

The angel Gabriel then gave Daniel one of the most outstanding prophecies of the whole Old Testament. It came to Daniel as a result of his heart and longing to understand what would happen to his people. This prophecy reflects God's love and faithfulness to Daniel. It gave him great hope and courage at the end of his long life of devotion to God. Here is the prophecy:

Daniel 9:24-27 Lamsa
Seventy times seven weeks are determined upon your people and upon your holy city, to finish the transgressions and to make an end of sins and for the forgiveness of the iniquity and to bring in

*everlasting righteousness and to fulfill the vision of the prophets
and to give the most holy to Messiah.*
*Know therefore and understand that from the going forth of the
word to restore and build Jerusalem to the coming of the Messiah
the king shall be seven times seven weeks, and sixty-two times
seven weeks; the people shall return and build Jerusalem, its
streets, and its broad ways at the end of the appointed times.*
*After sixty-two times seven weeks, Messiah shall be slain, and the
city shall be without a ruler; and the holy city shall be destroyed
together with the coming king; and the end thereof shall be a mass
exile, and at the end of the war, desolations are determined.*
*And he shall confirm the covenant with many for seven weeks and
half of seven weeks, then he shall cause the sacrifice and gift offerings to cease, and upon the horns of the altar the abomination of
desolation; and the desolation shall continue until the end of the
appointed time; the city shall remain desolate.*

This prophecy of the seventy weeks has to be one of the most con-
troversial sections of all of scripture. Rather than give all of the var-
ied interpretations, I will provide a very simple solution of how to
understand the timetable presented in these verses.

First, the Hebrew word *shabua* means "sevens" or "sevened" and this can refer to actual days (such as in a week) or years. In this case, it is referring to years. God is speaking of seventy times seven (70 x 7) years or 490 years. This time period concerning Israel was to

"Weeks" can stand for years and "time" for a year in prophecy

begin with "the going forth of the word to restore and build Jerusalem" as Lamsa translates it. There are actually several decrees which
have the potential to be what is mentioned here, but the only one
that fits the parameters of 483 years to the coming of the Messiah is
the decree of Artaxerxes in Ezra 7:11-26. This is usually stated to

have happened in 457 B.C., with some scholars choosing 458 B.C. instead.

The time period of 490 is further divided into three sections: 7 weeks of years (49 years), 62 weeks of years (434 years) and 1 week of years (7 years). Furthermore, the last week of years is divided into two parts—3½ years and 3½ years.

There are six promises in Daniel 9:24. Everlasting righteousness will be brought in and the most holy place anointed. Prophecy will be "sealed up." The fulfillment of these will "make atonement for iniquity" and this end of sin will occur at the time the Jews accept their Messiah and his earthly reign begins. Now the beginning point and the ending point of the 490 years is known.

Daniel 9:24 NASB
Seventy weeks have been decreed for your people and your holy city, to finish the transgression, to make an end of sin, to make atonement for iniquity, to bring in everlasting righteousness, to seal up vision and prophecy, and to anoint the most holy place.

Key Event	Date	Years	Total
Going forth of commandment	458 B.C.		
Restoration of Jerusalem	409 B.C.	49 years	49 years
Coming of the Messiah	27 A.D.	434 years	483 years
Rise of Antichrist	?	3½ years	486½ years
Israel's final cleansing	?	3½ years	490 years

The first section of 49 years is the period of time when Jerusalem "shall be built again with squares and moat, but in a troubled time" (Daniel 9:25 ESV). Counting 49 years from 458 B.C. bring us to 409 B.C. Prideaux, a secular historian, declared that Nehemiah's last action in rebuilding the city occurred in the 15th year of Darius Nothus (423-404 B.C.).[21] He actually uses the 409 B.C. date in his book which was published in 1715.

The second section counts sixty-two times seven (62 x 7) years (434) from 409 B.C. This covers the period from the completion of the work of rebuilding the city to "the anointed one," to the coming of the Messiah. There are two major ideas of when this point occurs: Jesus' baptism or his triumphal entry into Jerusalem. The first is more likely because the baptism is when he was "anointed" with the Holy Spirit. Choosing this endpoint for the 434 years brings us to 27 A.D. (counting only year between 1 B.C. and 1 A.D.). There are many scholars who agree that this is the beginning of Jesus' ministry.

There is continued controversy about when the last seven years end. As we have seen, it must end with the most holy place being restored. Some Jewish scholars even try to have the seventieth week end with the destruction of Jerusalem in 70 A.D. The most commonly held idea is that the last seven years begin with Christ's ministry and end about three and a half years after his death (see Anderson[22]). The problem with this theory is that there is no significant event recorded in the book of Acts that would mark the end of the period.

Two reasons for the controversy are: 1) the belief that Jesus' ministry was about three and a half years and 2) that the crucifixion was on a Friday which means it would need to have been in 30 A.D. There are two clear answers to this problem which then resolve all the controversy. First of all, although it is a rather current teaching,

---

[21] Prideaux, Humphrey. *The Old and New Testament Connected in the History of the Jews*, p. 499.
[22] Anderson, Sir Robert. *The Coming Prince*, p. 249-250.

there are more and more scholars who agree that Jesus' ministry was a little over a year. [23]

He needed to be "a lamb of the first year" in order to fulfill the requirement of the burnt offering. Also, he himself declares that the prophecy in Isaiah about the "acceptable year of the Lord" (KJV) is fulfilled when he announces the beginning of his ministry in Nazareth.

Luke 4:17-21 ESV
And the scroll of the prophet Isaiah was given to him. He unrolled the scroll and found the place where it was written,
"The Spirit of the Lord is upon me, because he has anointed me to proclaim good news to the poor. He has sent me to proclaim liberty to the captives and recovering of sight to the blind, to set at liberty those who are oppressed,
to proclaim the year of the Lord's favor."
And he rolled up the scroll and gave it back to the attendant and sat down. And the eyes of all in the synagogue were fixed on him. And he began to say to them, "Today this Scripture has been fulfilled in your hearing."

There are many of the early church fathers up until the fifth century who all believed that Jesus' ministry was a little over a year, including Basilides (120-140 A.D.), Origen (185-254), Tertullian (160-220?), Ephraem (306-373) and more. It was not until the time of Eusebius (260-340) when he convinced many others that Jesus' ministry was three and a half years.[24]

The second answer is that since Jesus' ministry was only a little over a year, the description in the Gospels of when Passover occurred (on

---

[23] Cummins, Walter, *The Acceptable Year of the Lord*, pp.48-50.
[24] *historical-jesus.info/appb.html*

a Wednesday) fits with the events as recorded in 28 A.D. In order for Jesus to have been in the grave for three literal days and nights, the crucifixion cannot be on Friday.

This now leaves the last week of the seventy weeks. The NLT version of Daniel 9:26 says, *"After this period of sixty-two sets of seven, the Anointed One will be killed, appearing to have accomplished nothing, and a ruler will arise whose armies will destroy the city and the Temple. The end will come with a flood, and war and its miseries are decreed from that time to the very end."* Between the phrases "the Anointed One will be killed" and "a ruler will arise" is currently a gap of almost 2,000 years. This is the time period of the mystery as we already learned.

The ruler who will arise is none other than the Antichrist which we have described. At the beginning of the last seven years he makes a covenant with Daniel's people (Israel) and allows them to rebuild the temple and set up the offerings again. But in the middle of the last seven years (3½ years), he breaks the covenant with Israel and sets up "the abomination of desolation" in the temple.

The middle of the last seven years begins the time of the great tribulation which will be described in the next chapter. The days will become darker before Christ returns and destroys the Antichrist and his kingdom.

CHAPTER 5 ⚖ THE ABOMINATION OF DESOLATION

Events	Scriptures
Gospel is preached throughout the age	Matthew 24:14 Mark 13:9-13 Luke 21:12-19
Two witnesses	Revelation 11:4-12 Zechariah 4:12-14
Abomination of desolation set up in middle of 7th week	Daniel 8:9-14 Daniel 9:27; 11:31; 12:11
Antichrist displays himself as God	2 Thessalonians 2:3-5
Great tribulation begins	Matthew 24:15-26 Mark 13:14-20 Luke 21:20-21
Strong delusion	2 Thessalonians 2:8-12

THE GOSPEL IS PREACHED

We have an interlude verse in the discussion in Matthew between the beginning of sorrows and the description of the great tribulation. The Gospel of the kingdom will be preached throughout this whole time period and many will be saved. And many will be persecuted for the choice of not embracing the rise of the Antichrist.

Matthew 24:14 APNT
And this gospel of the kingdom will be preached in the entire world for a testimony to all of the nations and then the end will come.

Mark 13:9-13 APNT
But watch out for yourselves, for they will deliver you to the judges, and in the synagogues you will be beaten, and you will stand before kings and governors because of me, as a testimony to them.

THE ABOMINATION OF DESOLATION

But first my gospel will be preached among all the nations.
And when they bring you to deliver you up, do not be anxious be-
forehand about what you will say or think, but what is given to you
at that moment, that speak. For you are not speaking, but the Holy
Spirit.
And brother will deliver his brother to death and a father his son
and children will rise up against their parents and will put them to
death.
And you will be hated by all men because of my name. But he who
endures until the end will live.

O━

The Gospel continues to be preached
throughout the end times

Luke 21:12-19 APNT
But before all these [things], they will lay hands on you and perse-
cute you and deliver you to the synagogues and to prison, and they
will bring you before kings and governors on account of my name.
But it will happen to you for a testimony.
And put [it] in your heart[s] that you should not be learning to
make a defense,
for I will give to you a mouth and wisdom so that all your enemies
will not be able to stand against it.
And your fathers and your brothers and your kinsmen and your
friends will betray you and they will kill some of you.
And you will be hated by everyone on account of my name,
yet not a hair from your head will be hurt.
And by your patience you will gain your life.

In Revelation 11, there are two witnesses who are especially called
to preach the gospel during this time. It says that they preach for
1,260 days and that they are two persons referred to as "olive trees

and candlesticks." This period of 1,260 days does not necessarily have to coincide with the first or last half of the seventh week. They could start preaching earlier than when the abomination is set up and finish before the end of the tribulation. The setting in Revelation is after the sixth trumpet and between the second and third woes.

Revelation 11:3-4 KJV
And I will give power unto my two witnesses, and they shall prophesy a thousand two hundred and threescore days, clothed in sackcloth.
These are the two olive trees, and the two candlesticks standing before the God of the earth.

This is a metaphor which was similarly used in Zechariah. These two witnesses are given power by God to witness throughout this time.

Zechariah 4:12-14 NASB
And I answered the second time and said to him, "What are the two olive branches which are beside the two golden pipes, which empty the golden oil from themselves?"
So he answered me saying, "Do you not know what these are?"
And I said, "No, my lord."
Then he said, "These are the two anointed ones, who are standing by the Lord of the whole earth."

Ephrem the Syrian, one of the early Church fathers, believed that these two witnesses would be literally Enoch and Elijah. Dr. Ken Johnson compiled writings on the end times by the early fathers and speaks about Ephrem:

> He agrees with Irenaeus on a pre-trib rapture. He, like the rest of the fathers, taught the two witnesses would be literally Enoch and Elijah physically returning to earth; or,

as John the Baptist came in the spirit and power of Elijah, so two modern Jews will be anointed in the spirit and power of Enoch and Elijah. Either way, the two witnesses are consistently referred to as Enoch and Elijah.[25]

The Gospel continues to be preached with boldness despite the intensity of the persecution of the believers. It is not clear who these two witnesses are but they certainly have specific powers and instructions. And it is also clear that God makes sure the Gospel is preached as Jesus described in Matthew 24.

Revelation 11:5-6 KJV
And if any man will hurt them, fire proceedeth out of their mouth, and devoureth their enemies: and if any man will hurt them, he must in this manner be killed. These have power to shut heaven, that it rain not in the days of their prophecy: and have power over waters to turn them to blood, and to smite the earth with all plagues, as often as they will.

The Antichrist attacks and kills them and possibly uses their deaths to even further consolidate his power.[26]

Revelation 11:7-14 ESV
And when they have finished their testimony, the beast that rises from the bottomless pit will make war on them and conquer them and kill them,
and their dead bodies will lie in the street of the great city that symbolically is called Sodom and Egypt, where their Lord was crucified.

[25] Johnson, Ken. *The End-Times by the Ancient Church Fathers,* p. 33.
[26] Martin, Ernest. *The Life and Times of the Antichrist,* pp. 7-8.

THE ABOMINATION OF DESOLATION

*For three and a half days some from the peoples and tribes and
languages and nations will gaze at their dead bodies and refuse to
let them be placed in a tomb,
and those who dwell on the earth will rejoice over them and make
merry and exchange presents, because these two prophets had
been a torment to those who dwell on the earth.
But after the three and a half days a breath of life from God entered them, and they stood up on their feet, and great fear fell on
those who saw them.
Then they heard a loud voice from heaven saying to them, "Come
up here!" And they went up to heaven in a cloud, and their enemies watched them.
And at that hour there was a great earthquake, and a tenth of the
city fell. Seven thousand people were killed in the earthquake, and
the rest were terrified and gave glory to the God of heaven.
The second woe has passed; behold, the third woe is soon to come.*

THE ABOMINATION OF DESOLATION

There are four references to an "abomination of desolation" in Daniel. As we saw in the previous chapter, some of the prophecies in
Daniel were fulfilled in the person of Antiochus IV. In Daniel 8 he
is introduced as the little horn.

Daniel 8:9-12 NIV
*Out of one of them came another horn, which started small but
grew in power to the south and to the east and toward the Beautiful Land.
It grew until it reached the host of the heavens, and it threw some
of the starry host down to the earth and trampled on them.
It set itself up to be as great as the commander of the army of the
LORD; it took away the daily sacrifice from the LORD, and his
sanctuary was thrown down.*

THE ABOMINATION OF DESOLATION

Because of rebellion, the LORD's people and the daily sacrifice were given over to it. It prospered in everything it did, and truth was thrown to the ground.

Once Antiochus came into power, he set up an idolatrous altar in the temple. This took place in 167 B.C. Then Daniel records a holy one speaking, asking how long the temple would be desecrated.

Daniel 8:13-14 NIV
Then I heard a holy one speaking, and another holy one said to him, "How long will it take for the vision to be fulfilled– the vision concerning the daily sacrifice, the rebellion that causes desolation, the surrender of the sanctuary and the trampling underfoot of the LORD's people?"
He said to me, "It will take 2,300 evenings and mornings; then the sanctuary will be reconsecrated."

The prophecy in Daniel 8 is explained by Gabriel and he tells him that it refers to the appointed time of the end. The 2,300 evenings and mornings are the two sacrifices on 1,150 days. This was fulfilled when Judas Maccabaeus rededicated the temple in 164 B.C. But it also refers to a similar time period within the last seventh week which will also be as precise.[27]

In verse 13 there is the first reference to the abomination of desolation. Here it is called "the rebellion that causes desolation." But the ESV is a little clearer, calling it "the transgression that makes desolate." The word "desolate" is from the Hebrew verb *shamem* (Strong's #8074) and means "to be stunned, appalling, causing horror" as it is used in the Polel tense. This tense puts stress

---

[27] www.biblearchaeology.org: Understanding the 2,300 "Evenings and Mornings" of Daniel-8:14

on the fact that someone (or something) has caused the sanctuary to become polluted and thus unfit for the worship and service of God.[28]

The second reference in Daniel is from chapter 9 which we studied before.

Daniel 9:27 TNK
During one week he will make a firm covenant with many. For half a week he will put a stop to the sacrifice and the meal offering. At the corner of the altar will be an appalling abomination until the decreed destruction will be poured down upon the appalling thing.

The word translated "corner" in the Tanakh is the Hebrew word for wing. There is an ellipsis following to insert something about the temple. It could be inserted as follows: "on the wing (of the sacred edifice or temple) there will be filthiness, even a desolator." When the verb *shamem* is used as a noun it could be translated "desolator" or "horror-causer." From this verse, we learn that the desecration will definitely happen in the temple, perhaps at the altar.

The third use of desolation in Daniel is equally as explicit.

Daniel 11:31 NET
His forces will rise up and profane the fortified sanctuary, stopping the daily sacrifice. In its place they will set up the abomination that causes desolation.

From a study of the usage of the word "abomination," it is found that it is strongly related to idols and idolatry. *The International Standard Bible Encyclopedia* explains that the Hebrew word *shiqquts* is used to describe specific forms of idolatrous worship

---

[28] Harris, Archer, Waltke, eds. *Theological Wordbook of the Old Testament,* p. 937.

which were especially abhorrent. So this verse definitely refers not only to Antiochus IV, but to a future desecrator of the temple.

> When Daniel undertook to specify an abomination so sur-passing disgusting to the sense of morality and decency, and so aggressive against everything that was godly as to drive all from its presence and leave its abode desolate, he chose this as the strongest among the several synonyms...[29]

It is not clear exactly what the abomination is or where in the temple it is set up. What is known is that public worship of the true God (the daily sacrifice and oblation) is taken away and the sanctuary is defiled. There is an image which the false prophet has made to the beast. The false prophet has the power to give life (*pneuma*) to the image of the beast so that it speaks, causing people to worship it. 2 Thessalonians describes the Antichrist's purpose for setting up the abomination in the temple. That is where the Antichrist takes his seat as God.

2 Thessalonians 2:3-5 NASB
Let no one in any way deceive you, for it will not come unless the apostasy comes first, and the man of lawlessness is revealed, the son of destruction,
who opposes and exalts himself above every so-called god or ob-ject of worship, so that he takes his seat in the temple of God, dis-playing himself as being God.
Do you not remember that while I was still with you, I was telling you these things?

The last verse about the abomination in Daniel is very similar to the previous verse, but also mentions several new specific time periods.

---

[29] Orr, James ed, *The International Standard Bible Encyclopedia,* Vol I., p. 16.

THE ABOMINATION OF DESOLATION

Daniel 12:11-12 NLT
From the time the daily sacrifice is stopped and the sacrilegious
object that causes desecration is set up to be worshiped, there will
be 1,290 days.
And blessed are those who wait and remain until the end of the
1,335 days!

We do not know exactly what these additional 45 days are but it definitely is implied that there are blessings at the end of the 1,335 days! As we will see in future chapters, after Jesus Christ returns, there are still some events before the kingdom is set up.

In the Mount of Olives discourse when Jesus was teaching his disciples about the end times, he states that the next event after the beginning of sorrows is this setting up of the abomination that causes desolation. The Aramaic translation of the phrase is literally, "the abominable sign of desecration." This is an important turning point in our timeline of the events of the end times.

Matthew 24:15-26 ESV
So when you see the abomination of desolation spoken of by the
prophet Daniel, standing in the holy place (let the reader under-
stand),
then let those who are in Judea flee to the mountains.
Let the one who is on the housetop not go down to take what is in
his house,
and let the one who is in the field not turn back to take his cloak.
And alas for women who are pregnant and for those who are nurs-
ing infants in those days!
Pray that your flight may not be in winter or on a Sabbath.
For then there will be great tribulation, such as has not been from
the beginning of the world until now, no, and never will be.
And if those days had not been cut short, no human being would be
saved. But for the sake of the elect those days will be cut short.

THE ABOMINATION OF DESOLATION

Then if anyone says to you, 'Look, here is the Christ!' or 'There he is!' do not believe it.
For false christs and false prophets will arise and perform great signs and wonders, so as to lead astray, if possible, even the elect.
See, I have told you beforehand.
So, if they say to you, 'Look, he is in the wilderness,' do not go out.
If they say, 'Look, he is in the inner rooms,' do not believe it.

The exhortation to flee is in all three of the Synoptic Gospels because this begins the time of the great tribulation. The word tribulation is sometimes translated as "ordeal, distress, persecution, anguish or trial." The Jewish believers are exhorted by Jesus Christ to flee to the mountains after they see the abomination set up.

Mark 13:14 ISV
So when you see the destructive desecration standing where it should not be (let the reader take note), then those who are in Judea must flee to the mountains.

The powerful lying signs and wonders done by the false trinity of the Dragon, the beast and the false prophet will definitely delude many.

2 Thessalonians 2:8-12 NASB
And then that lawless one will be revealed whom the Lord will slay with the breath of His mouth and bring to an end by the appearance of His coming;
that is, the one whose coming is in accord with the activity of Satan, with all power and signs and false wonders,
and with all the deception of wickedness for those who perish, because they did not receive the love of the truth so as to be saved.
And for this reason God will send upon them a deluding influence so that they might believe what is false,

69

in order that they all may be judged who did not believe the truth, but took pleasure in wickedness.

Things are getting darker and darker. There still remains 1,260 days which will be the worst days that mankind has ever had to endure. But the arrival of Christ to set it all right is coming quickly!

CHAPTER 6 ⚕ THE GREAT TRIBULATION

Events	Scriptures
Mark of the beast	Revelation 13:17-18
5th seal	Revelation 6:9-11
	Luke 19:43-44
1,260 days or 42 months	Revelation 11:2-3
Day of Jacob's trouble	Jeremiah 30:7
	Daniel 12:11
	Habakkuk 3:16
Day of their calamity	Obadiah 1:13-14
Day of visitation	Isaiah 10:3-7
Indignation	Isaiah 10:24-27
	Daniel 11:36

The Antichrist causes all those who will not worship the image of the beast to be killed. They must receive a mark, and without this mark, they cannot buy or sell.

Revelation 13:17-18 KJV
And that no man might buy or sell, save he that had the mark, or the name of the beast, or the number of his name.
Here is wisdom. Let him that hath understanding count the number of the beast: for it is the number of a man; and his number is Six hundred threescore and six.

Now it is easy to understand the opening of the fifth seal in Revelation 6:9-11.

Revelation 6:9-11 NASB
And when He broke the fifth seal, I saw underneath the altar the souls of those who had been slain because of the word of God, and because of the testimony which they had maintained;

and they cried out with a loud voice, saying, "How long, O Lord, holy and true, wilt Thou refrain from judging and avenging our blood on those who dwell on the earth?"
And there was given to each of them a white robe; and they were told that they should rest for a little while longer, until the number of their fellow servants and their brethren who were to be killed even as they had been, should be completed also.

There are many believers who are killed during this time. There is a "great multitude" of people of every nation who do believe and refuse to worship the beast. Jerusalem is the focus of the persecution, although believers are scattered throughout the world.

Luke 21:23 tells us that "there shall be great distress in the land and wrath upon this people" which culminates in people in Israel dying or being led away captive into all nations. This was partially fulfilled in the destruction of Jerusalem in 70 A.D., but there will be a future fulfillment also.

The setting up of the abomination "in the middle of the week" begins the 3½ year period of the great tribulation. The phrases used in the books of Daniel and Revelation which define these 3½ years are: "time and times and the dividing of time"(Daniel 7:25); "time, times, and a half" (Daniel 12:7); "forty and two months" (Revelation 11:2); "a thousand two hundred and threescore (1,260) days" (Revelation 11:3).

DAY OF...

The phrases "day of" and "time of" describe this time period of intense persecution and if God did not shorten it, no one would survive.

THE GREAT TRIBULATION

Mark 13:19-20 KJV
For in those days shall be affliction, such as was not from the be-
ginning of the creation which God created unto this time, neither
shall be.
And except that the Lord had shortened those days, no flesh should
be saved: but for the elect's sake, whom he hath chosen, he hath
shortened the days.

It is called "a time of distress for Jacob."

Jeremiah 30:7 ESV
Alas! That day is so great there is none like it; it is a time of dis-
tress for Jacob; yet he shall be saved out of it.

Daniel 12:1 ESV
At that time shall arise Michael, the great prince who has charge
of your people. And there shall be a time of trouble, such as never
has been since there was a nation till that time. But at that time
your people shall be delivered, everyone whose name shall be
found written in the book.

Habakkuk got a vision of this time of tribulation also.

Habakkuk 3:16 ESV
I hear, and my body trembles; my lips quiver at the sound; rotten-
ness enters into my bones; my legs tremble beneath me. Yet I will
quietly wait for the day of trouble to come upon people who invade
us.

It is also called the "day of their calamity." Calamity and distress
are the same word, *tsarah*, which we have seen can be translated as
tribulation.

THE GREAT TRIBULATION

Obadiah 1:13-14 ESV
Do not enter the gate of my people in the day of their calamity; do
not gloat over his disaster in the day of his calamity; do not loot
his wealth in the day of his calamity.
Do not stand at the crossroads to cut off his fugitives; do not hand
over his survivors in the day of distress.

Isaiah 10 has a whole section that describes what happens when the
"Assyrian," as the Antichrist is called, visits God's people with
intense persecution. This prophecy was partially fulfilled when
Assyria took the ten northern tribes of Israel into captivity, but it
also has a future fulfillment.

Isaiah 10:3-7 KJV
And what will ye do in the day of visitation, and in the desolation
which shall come from far? to whom will ye flee for help? and
where will ye leave your glory?
Without me they shall bow down under the prisoners, and they
shall fall under the slain. For all this his anger is not turned away,
but his hand is stretched out still.
O Assyrian, the rod of mine anger, and the staff in their hand is
mine indignation.
I will send him against an hypocritical nation, and against the peo-
ple of my wrath will I give him a charge, to take the spoil, and to
take the prey, and to tread them down like the mire of the streets.
Howbeit he meaneth not so, neither doth his heart think so; but it
is in his heart to destroy and cut off nations not a few.

Later in the chapter, there is comfort for Israel that the Assyrian's
reign will be cut off after the "indignation" is complete. This "indignation" used here and in other verses refers to the punishment of
Israel for its unbelief.

THE GREAT TRIBULATION

Isaiah 10:24-25 NASB
Therefore thus says the Lord God of hosts, "O My people who
dwell in Zion, do not fear the Assyrian who strikes you with the rod
and lifts up his staff against you, the way Egypt did.
For in a very little while My indignation against you will be spent,
and My anger will be directed to their destruction."

Daniel 11:36 NASB
Then the king will do as he pleases, and he will exalt and magnify
himself above every god, and will speak monstrous things against
the God of gods; and he will prosper until the indignation is fin-
ished, for that which is decreed will be done.

The indignation is going to be finished soon. Now is the time for the
breaking of the sixth seal and the ushering in of the day of the Lord.
We can take a deep breath and ask, "How much longer will it be?"

Zephaniah 1:14-18 ESV
The great day of the Lord is near, near and hastening fast; the
sound of the day of the Lord is bitter; the mighty man cries aloud
there.
A day of wrath is that day, a day of distress and anguish, a day of
ruin and devastation, a day of darkness and gloom, a day of clouds
and thick darkness,
a day of trumpet blast and battle cry against the fortified cities and
against the lofty battlements.
I will bring distress on mankind, so that they shall walk like the
blind, because they have sinned against the LORD; their blood
shall be poured out like dust, and their flesh like dung.
Neither their silver nor their gold shall be able to deliver them on
the day of the wrath of the LORD. In the fire of his jealousy, all the
earth shall be consumed; for a full and sudden end he will make of
all the inhabitants of the earth.

CHAPTER 7 ⚖ THE DAY OF THE LORD BEGINS

Events	Scriptures
Great signs	Matthew 24:29
Sun and moon darkened, stars fall	Mark 13:24-25
Powers of heaven are shaken	Luke 21:25-26
Moon turned to blood	Joel 2:10-11, 31
	Isaiah 13:9-13
	Ezekiel 32:7-8
	Acts 2:19-20
6th seal	Revelation 6:12-16
Earthquake	
144,000 sealed	Revelation 7:1-8
The day of the Lord begins	Acts 2:20

At the height of the intensity of the persecution, God goes into action to turn the tide against the Evil One and his Antichrist. All of a sudden, there are spectacular signs in the heavens.

Matthew 24:29 KJV
Immediately after the tribulation of those days shall the sun be darkened, and the moon shall not give her light, and the stars shall fall from heaven, and the powers of the heavens shall be shaken.

Mark 13:24-25 ESV
But in those days, after that tribulation, the sun will be darkened, and the moon will not give its light,
and the stars will be falling from heaven, and the powers in the heavens will be shaken.

The people respond with perplexity and fear because of the signs.

THE DAY OF THE LORD BEGINS

Luke 21:25-26 ESV
And there will be signs in sun and moon and stars, and on the earth distress of nations in perplexity because of the roaring of the sea and the waves,
people fainting with fear and with foreboding of what is coming on the world. For the powers of the heavens will be shaken.

The signs are revealed with the opening of the sixth seal in Revelation 6:12-16.

Revelation 6:12-14 KJV
And I beheld when he had opened the sixth seal, and, lo, there was a great earthquake; and the sun became black as sackcloth of hair, and the moon became as blood;

> *Great signs announce the beginning of the day of the Lord*

And the stars of heaven fell unto the earth, even as a fig tree casteth her untimely figs, when she is shaken of a mighty wind.
And the heaven departed as a scroll when it is rolled together; and every mountain and island were moved out of their places.

These signs of upheaval in the earth are described in the Old Testament also.

Joel 2:10-11 ESV
The earth quakes before them; the heavens tremble. The sun and the moon are darkened, and the stars withdraw their shining.
The LORD utters his voice before his army, for his camp is exceedingly great; he who executes his word is powerful. For the day of the Lord is great and very awesome; who can endure it?

These signs usher in the fury of the wrath of God and the day of the Lord.

THE DAY OF THE LORD BEGINS

Isaiah 13:9-13 ESV
Behold, the day of the Lord comes, cruel, with wrath and fierce anger, to make the land a desolation and to destroy its sinners from it.
For the stars of the heavens and their constellations will not give their light; the sun will be dark at its rising, and the moon will not shed its light.
I will punish the world for its evil, and the wicked for their iniquity; I will put an end to the pomp of the arrogant, and lay low the pompous pride of the ruthless.
I will make people more rare than fine gold, and mankind than the gold of Ophir.
Therefore I will make the heavens tremble, and the earth will be shaken out of its place, at the wrath of the LORD of hosts in the day of his fierce anger.

These signs will be so astounding that people will be awakened to the fact that something is going on and is changing. None of the blood moons which have happened recently came even close to this description!

Ezekiel 32:7-8 ESV
When I blot you out, I will cover the heavens and make their stars dark; I will cover the sun with a cloud, and the moon shall not give its light.
All the bright lights of heaven will I make dark over you, and put darkness on your land, declares the Lord GOD.

Acts declares that these great signs announce the day of the Lord.

Acts 2:19-20 KJV
And I will shew wonders in heaven above, and signs in the earth beneath; blood, and fire, and vapour of smoke:

THE DAY OF THE LORD BEGINS

The sun shall be turned into darkness, and the moon into blood, before that great and notable day of the Lord come:

These wonders begin the "terrible" day of the Lord. The day of the Lord is the time period when the Lord Jehovah does the judging and his justice on the unbelievers is poured out. But before the details of the day of the Lord unfold, we see that God does something extremely remarkable. He "seals" a special group of people who will be able to endure the wrath and will evangelize during this time.

THE SEALING OF THE 144,000

The sealing of the 144,000 is recorded in Revelation 7:1-8.

Revelation 7:1-4 KJV
And after these things I saw four angels standing on the four corners of the earth, holding the four winds of the earth, that the wind should not blow on the earth, nor on the sea, nor on any tree.
And I saw another angel ascending from the east, having the seal of the living God: and he cried with a loud voice to the four angels, to whom it was given to hurt the earth and the sea,
Saying, Hurt not the earth, neither the sea, nor the trees, till we have sealed the servants of our God in their foreheads.
And I heard the number of them which were sealed: and there were sealed an hundred and forty and four thousand of all the tribes of the children of Israel.

This sealing is the answer to the question in Revelation 6:17 of who shall be able to stand when the great day of his wrath is come. It is God choosing out an elect remnant which will be able to pass through all of the rest of the tribulation. This is similar to the seven thousand that God knew had not bowed their knees to Baal during the days of Elijah.

79

John Walvoord in his book on *The Revelation of Jesus Christ* explains this sealing as follows:

> The implication is that the judgment of God is impending and that prior to its infliction on the earth, God wants to set apart and protect His servants....It is implied that these who are thus sealed have been saved in the time of trouble pictured in the book of Revelation and by this means are being set apart as a special divine remnant to be a testimony to God's grace and mercy during this time of judgment.[30]

The criteria for receiving the seal are explained in Revelation 14. They do not follow the "lie" or the idolatry of the time. The seal is their Father's name written in their foreheads. There are 12,000 out of each tribe (note the omission of Dan and Ephraim), and they are the "firstfruits unto God and to the Lamb."

Revelation 14:4-5 NASB
These are the ones who have not been defiled with women, for they have kept themselves chaste. These are the ones who follow the Lamb wherever He goes. These have been purchased from among men as first fruits to God and to the Lamb.
And no lie was found in their mouth; they are blameless.

There is not much information except for these verses about this group of people. The key point to understand is that they are firstfruits to God and the Lamb. They will be on the top of Mount Zion when Jesus Christ returns to the earth. They are called "the purchased ones."

---

[30] Walvoord, John. *The Revelation of Jesus Christ*, p. 140.

THE DAY OF THE LORD BEGINS

Revelation 14:1-3 APNT
And I saw, and behold, a lamb was standing on the mountain of
Zion and with him [were] one hundred and forty-four thousand
who had his name and the name of his Father written on their
foreheads.
And I heard a sound from heaven as the sound of many waters and
as the sound of great thunder. The sound that I heard [was] as a
harpist who strikes on his harps.
And they were praising as a new praise song before the throne and
before the four living creatures and before the elders. And no one
was able to learn the praise song, except the one hundred and
forty-four thousand purchased [ones] from the earth.

THE DAY OF THE LORD

It is important to understand the overall time period of the day of the
Lord before we look at the details of the seventh seal.

The Lord Jehovah (or Yahweh) does the judging during the "day of
the Lord." This must always be kept in mind when reading this
phrase. Within the context of the first use of the "day of the Lord,"
there are two crucial points. Each point is presented twice and thus
established with emphasis. The first point is that all those who are
proud and lofty (the unbelievers) will be humbled and Jehovah will
be exalted in the day of the Lord.

Isaiah 2:11-12 NET
Proud men will be brought low, arrogant men will be humiliated;
the LORD alone will be exalted in that day.
Indeed, the LORD who commands armies has planned a day of
judgment, for all the high and mighty, for all who are proud— they
will be humiliated;

THE DAY OF THE LORD BEGINS

The day of the Lord is a time period in which all the events have one major purpose, to praise and honor Jehovah God. God is exalted and unbelievers are humbled. This is a successive development as the events unfold. It is important to note that verse 12 specifically says that the day of the Lord is directed toward *unbelievers*. It is a time of God's judgments on prideful and haughty men. Verse 17 repeats the same thought.

Isaiah 2:17 NET
Proud men will be humiliated, arrogant men will be brought low; the LORD alone will be exalted in that day.

The second point that is repeated is in Isaiah 2:19-21. When the day of the Lord comes, the unbelievers will flee to the rocks and caves "for fear of the Lord, and for the glory of his majesty, when he ariseth to shake terribly the earth" (Isaiah 2:19b, repeated in verse 21b). The day of the Lord is the time when God sets the record straight that HE is the one true God who alone should be worshipped and exalted. The glory of his majesty will be in evidence. All of God's wrath will be poured out during those days on the unbelievers and on the whole earth. It will be a fearful and terrible time in which to live. By the end of the day of the Lord, all of God's judgments will have been spoken and his sentences pronounced and carried out. His "divine intervention" will be complete and God will personally be in charge of all the courses of action.

The day of the Lord has one major purpose – to praise and honor God

With these two points in mind, let us look at the uses in the New Testament to discover the time framework. The "day of the Lord" is used five times in the New Testament: once in Acts, twice in Thessalonians, once in Peter and once in Revelation.

THE DAY OF THE LORD BEGINS

Acts 2:20 reveals when the day of the Lord begins in the sequence of the events of the end times.

Acts 2:20 KJV
The sun shall be turned into darkness, and the moon into blood,
before that great and notable day of the Lord come:

"Before" is the Greek word *prin*. Thayer defines it as "before, before that: ... with an aorist infinitive having the force of the Latin future perfect, of things future."[31] The word "come" in Acts 2:20 is an aorist infinitive. With this explanation, Acts 2:20b could be translated "before that great and notable day of the Lord shall have come." What is before that day? At least two signs are mentioned here as being before the day of the Lord. They are the sun turning into darkness and the moon turning into blood. As we have seen, these signs precede the pouring out of the wrath of God in the seventh seal. Thus the day of the Lord begins with the seventh seal. In terms of the order of events, the great tribulation is not a part the day of the Lord. Rather, the tribulation precedes the great signs which then usher in the day of the Lord.

This verse in Acts is quoted from Joel 2:31. The phrase to describe the day of the Lord in Acts is "great and notable," whereas in Joel it is "great and terrible." How do these two apparently different words fit together? The Greek word does mean notable and this agrees with the Septuagint version of Joel. However, the Aramaic word in Acts is *dehila* which means "fearful, formidable, terrible, dreadful awful.[32] This word lines up with the Hebrew word for terrible, *yare*. The Hebrew word *yare* can be translated either "fearful, dreadful or awful" or "to inspire reverence, godly fear or awe." Either trans-

---

[31] Thayer, Joseph Henry. *The New Thayer's Greek-English Lexicon,* p. 536.
[32] Smith, J. Payne. *A Compendious Syriac Dictionary*, p. 89.

lation would be accurate. The day of the Lord will be terrible and it will also be noteworthy.

Joel 2:11 KJV
And the Lord shall utter his voice before his army, for his camp is very great: for he is strong that executeth his word: for the day of the Lord is great and very terrible [yare] and who can abide it?

Malachi 4:5 ESV
Behold, I will send you Elijah the prophet before the great and awesome [yare] day of the LORD comes.

The second use of day of the Lord in the New Testament is in 1 Thessalonians. It begins to add more insight into the description of the time period.

1 Thessalonians 5:2-3 APNT
For you know truly that the day of our Lord will so come as a thief in the night,
when they say, "Peace and harmony." And then suddenly, destruction will come on them as birth pains on a pregnant woman and they will not escape.

There are two images used in this passage, that of the thief in the night and of a pregnant woman in travail. Both emphasize that suddenly or unexpectedly the day of the Lord will come. Then once it comes, there is no turning back or escape. A thief coming in the night is unforeseen. He stealthily comes to steal and rob and his visit brings ruin. A woman who is pregnant does not know when she will go into labor. The time when it comes is sudden and at that point, there is no stopping the process of birth. She must go through the travail. There is no escape.

1 Thessalonians 5:3 says, "when they say, Peace and harmony...." The "they" in this verse refers to the unbelievers who are prospering from the reign of the Antichrist. His reign will have brought in peace from wars and a security for those who have followed him and worshipped the image of the beast. The unbelievers confidently affirm that all is going well, but sudden destruction will befall them.

The word for "destruction" in 1 Thessalonians 5:3 is the Greek word *olethros*. Bullinger defines it as "ruin, death; that which causes death, ruin to others." The Hebrew word in the Old Testament passages pertaining to the day of the Lord is *shod*, which also means "devastation or ruin." Isaiah 13:6 and Joel 1:15 tell of this destruction.

Isaiah 13:6 ESV
Wail, for the day of the LORD is near; as destruction from the Almighty it will come!

Joel 1:15 ESV
Alas for the day! For the day of the LORD is near, and as destruction from the Almighty it comes.

One definition of *shod* from Brown, Driver, Briggs Lexicon is "desolation destruction, specially a devastating tempest." They translate Isaiah 13:6 as: "like a tempest shall it (suddenly) come from the Almighty."[33] However, there is more depth to the word than this. The meaning of the word also includes violence, spoil and ruin.

This picture is vivid when the Aramaic word for "comes upon" in 1 Thessalonians 5:3 is studied. It is the Aramaic word *qam* with the

---

[33] Brown, Francis, *The New Brown Driver Briggs Gesenius Hebrew and English Lexicon*, p. 994.

preposition 'al. The Payne Smith Lexicon defines this particular usage of the verb as "to stand opposite, rise or break against (as a storm or persecution)."[34] The Murdock translation from the Aramaic is "will burst upon them."

This ruin and devastation will suddenly break against the unbelievers (when they are saying "peace and safety"). The word for "escape" in 1 Thessalonians 5:3 is *ekpheugo* in Greek. It means "to flee out of, flee away, to seek safety in flight, to escape.[35] It will not be possible to escape any of the events of the day of the Lord!

In short summation of this section in 1 Thessalonians, there are several repeated images. The thief and the woman in travail are used to show the suddenness and unexpectedness of the day of the Lord. Furthermore, as the unbelievers are resting in their security, unanticipated destruction will break against them (as a tempest), laying the land and people desolate. There is no escape!

2 Thessalonians 2:2 is the next use of "day of the Lord" in the New Testament. The King James Version reads "day of Christ" but the other Greek and Aramaic texts have "day of the Lord." To fit with the context this verse should read "day of the Lord."

2 Thessalonians 2:1-3 APNT
Now we beg you, my brothers, concerning the coming of our Lord Jesus Christ and concerning our own gathering to him,
that you should not be quickly shaken in your minds, nor be troubled, not by word, nor by a spirit, nor by a letter, as though from us, [saying] namely, "Behold, the day of our Lord has arrived."

---

[34] Smith, J. Payne. *A Compendious Syriac Dictionary*, p. 494.
[35] Thayer, Joseph Henry. *The New Thayer's Greek-English Lexicon*, p. 200.

THE DAY OF THE LORD BEGINS

Will anyone deceive you in any way? Because [it will not come]
except a rebellion should come first and the man of sin should be
revealed, the son of destruction,

There are two phrases in verse 2 regarding the day of the Lord which
are noteworthy. They are "shaken in mind" and "troubled" and these
agree with the descriptions in the Old Testament. "Shaken" is the
Aramaic word *zaye* which is in the intensive tense. It means to be
"set in motion, shaken, affected disturbed, disquieted, terrified.[36]
The noun which comes from this verb in Aramaic is "earthquake."

Isaiah 13 describes this "shaken in mind" and again compares the
time of the day of the Lord as a woman who is giving birth.

Isaiah 13:7-8 KJV
Therefore shall all hands be faint, and every man's heart shall
melt:
And they shall be afraid: pangs and sorrows shall take hold of
them; they shall be in pain as a woman that travaileth: they shall
be amazed one at another; their faces shall be as flames.

When people are afraid, their faces radically change color. Amos
adds a detail that the people will be wailing also.

Amos 5:16-17 NET
Because of Israel's sins this is what the LORD, the God who com-
mands armies, the sovereign One, says: "In all the squares there
will be wailing, in all the streets they will mourn the dead. They
will tell the field workers to lament and the professional mourners
to wail.
In all the vineyards there will be wailing, for I will pass through
your midst," says the LORD.

---

[36] Smith, J. Payne. *A Compendious Syriac Dictionary*, p. 113.

THE DAY OF THE LORD BEGINS

The context of 2 Thessalonians 2 shows how the man of sin, the Antichrist, must be revealed before the day of the Lord comes. Again, this sets the timing of the day of the Lord to be after the Antichrist is in power, not at the beginning of the great tribulation.

It has been shown from Acts that the day of the Lord begins with great signs in the heavens followed by the wrath of God. The end point of the day of the Lord is defined in 2 Peter 3, which is the next use in the New Testament.

2 Peter 3:10 APNT
But the day of the LORD will come as a thief, in which the heaven[s] will suddenly pass away and the elements, while burning, will dissolve and the earth and the works that are in it will [not] be found.

The last events after the 1,000-year reign of Christ include the resurrection of the unjust and death being destroyed. The present heavens and earth are "dissolved" as the last thing to happen before the new heaven and earth. The context of 2 Peter 3 is about what will happen to this present heavens and earth.

2 Peter 3:7 KJV
But the heavens and the earth, which are now, by the same word are kept in store, reserved unto fire against the day of judgment and perdition of ungodly men.

When the last judgments of the ungodly men are finished, the fire of God will also "judge" the heavens and the earth and then all is finished to bring about the new heaven and earth and paradise. This is the end point of the day of the Lord when all the judging will be completed, "that God may be all in all" (1 Corinthians 15:28b). He will forever be the exalted one.

The fifth and final use is in Revelation 1. It identifies John as receiving revelation regarding the day of the Lord.

Revelation 1:10a KJV
I was in the spirit on the Lord's day....

John, like the Apostle Paul, had been "caught up" (2 Corinthians 12:4) or caught away to be spiritually in the middle of future events, specifically the day of the Lord. Revelation 1:10 describes the moment when God told John to write the book of Revelation. This use of the term "Lord's day" does not refer to Sunday, nor does it indicate that every event recorded in the book of Revelation is about the day of the Lord. Rather, as the day of the Lord was the context and focus of John's heart when he began writing the book, so it is the focus of the book itself.

Dwight Pentecost summarizes the timing of the day of the Lord like this:

> ...the day of the Lord" is an extensive time period which includes not only the tribulation and the judgments taking place at the second advent, but which includes also the entire millennial reign of Christ as a time period in which the Lord deals directly with human sin.[37]

The great signs of the earth, the sun turning dark and the moon turning to blood with powerful earthquakes, signal the beginning of the day of the Lord, as well as the beginning of the wrath of God.

As terrifying as the end time events will be, two points must be kept in mind. The first point is that the Church of the Body of Christ will not be part of the wrath to come.

---

[37] Walvoord, John, *The Millennial Kingdom*, p. 273.

1 Thessalonians 1:10 APNT
while you wait for his Son from heaven, Jesus, whom he raised from
the dead, who has delivered us from the wrath that is coming.

The second point is that the time of the reign of the Antichrist is
limited by God. As we have seen, he is really in power for only about
seven years. In a relatively short period of time, the beast and the
false prophet will be captured and cast into the lake of fire!

Now we will see what form the wrath of God will take in the seventh
seal, knowing it is time for it to be finished!

CHAPTER 8 ⚖ THE VENGEANCE AND WRATH OF GOD

Events	Scriptures
Day of wrath	Romans 1:18
	Isaiah 13:9
	Zephaniah 1:14-15
	Joel 2:1-3
	Amos 5:18-19
Day of vengeance	Luke 21:22-24
	Isaiah 61:2
7th seal	Revelation 8-11
	Revelation 16:1-12
Babylon is destroyed	Revelation 18

The focus of the wrath of God is on the worshippers of the beast. It is the fulfillment of the wrath of God as described in Romans 1:18.

Romans 1:18 NIV
The wrath of God is being revealed from heaven against all the godlessness and wickedness of people, who suppress the truth by their wickedness,

The time is coming when God will say, "That is enough!" The progression of events after that will be swift and the great day of the Lord will come to pass. Other uses of "day of the Lord" in the Old Testament spell out additional details about the kind of destruction that will occur and tie it in with the day of wrath.

Isaiah 13:9 NASB
Behold, the day of the LORD is coming, Cruel, with fury [ebrah] and burning anger, To make the land a desolation; And He will exterminate its sinners from it.

THE VENGEANCE AND WRATH OF GOD

The Hebrew word for "fury" is *ebrah* and emphasizes something that overflows. The day of wrath will be a fierce and complete demonstration of God's fury.

Zephaniah 1:14-15, 18 NASB
Near is the great day of the LORD, Near and coming very quickly;
Listen, the day of the LORD! In it the warrior cries out bitterly.
A day of wrath [ebrah] is that day, A day of trouble and distress, A
day of destruction and desolation, A day of darkness and gloom, A
day of clouds and thick darkness,
Neither their silver nor their gold will be able to deliver them on
the day of the LORD's wrath [ebrah]; And all the earth will be de-
voured in the fire of His jealousy, For He will make a complete
end, Indeed a terrifying one, Of all the inhabitants of the earth.

The earth will be devoured and there will be a complete end. This aspect of darkness is further emphasized in Joel.

Joel 2:1-2 ESV
Blow a trumpet in Zion; sound an alarm on my holy mountain! Let
all the inhabitants of the land tremble, for the day of the LORD is
coming; it is near,
a day of darkness and gloom, a day of clouds and thick darkness!
Like blackness there is spread upon the mountains a great and
powerful people; their like has never been before, nor will be
again after them through the years of all generations.

God's wrath sweeps away everything in its path, consuming all who have opposed him. Ezekiel compares this to silver melting in a furnace.

Ezekiel 22:21-22, 31 ESV
I will gather you and blow on you with the fire of my wrath
[ebrah], and you shall be melted in the midst of it.

THE VENGEANCE AND WRATH OF GOD

As silver is melted in a furnace, so you shall be melted in the midst of it, and you shall know that I am the LORD; I have poured out my wrath upon you."
Therefore I have poured out my indignation upon them. I have consumed them with the fire of my wrath [ebrah]. I have returned their way upon their heads, declares the Lord GOD.

Gold and silver will not deliver anyone in the day of wrath.

Ezekiel 7:19 ESV
They cast their silver into the streets, and their gold is like an unclean thing. Their silver and gold are not able to deliver them in the day of the wrath [ebrah] of the LORD. They cannot satisfy their hunger or fill their stomachs with it. For it was the stumbling block of their iniquity.

These are such specific descriptions of this time period. It will not be available to escape the desolation. Amos reveals again that it is a day of darkness, and verse 19 shows what will happen when the unbelievers try to flee.

Amos 5:18-20 ESV
Woe to you who desire the day of the LORD! Why would you have the day of the LORD? It is darkness, and not light,
as if a man fled from a lion, and a bear met him, or went into the house and leaned his hand against the wall, and a serpent bit him. Is not the day of the LORD darkness, and not light, and gloom with no brightness in it?

The "days of vengeance" will be completed during this time and even though many will be taken captive and Jerusalem will be trampled, once the times of the Gentiles is fulfilled, the distress will end with the coming of the true King and Messiah.

THE VENGEANCE AND WRATH OF GOD

Luke 21:22-24 NASB
because these are days of vengeance, in order that all things which are written may be fulfilled.
Woe to those who are with child and to those who nurse babes in those days; for there will be great distress upon the land, and wrath to this people,
and they will fall by the edge of the sword, and will be led captive into all the nations; and Jerusalem will be trampled under foot by the Gentiles until the times of the Gentiles be fulfilled.

The wrath of God is the seventh seal of the book of Revelation. It occupies the majority of all the visions in chapters 8-18. There are seven trumpets, the last three called woes, and the seventh trumpet is further divided into seven vials or bowls. They are consecutive in their occurrence and, by the end of this seventh seal at least a third part of the earth is killed.

The 144,000 are still alive at this point, and the persecution against them continues. This is evident because one of the bowls is locusts which have power to hurt those on the earth, but they are commanded not to hurt the trees and "only those men who have not the seal of God on their foreheads" (Revelation 9:4). The locusts have power to hurt men for five months. So this period of the wrath of God is at least five months, if not equal to what the Old Testament calls the "year of recompense."

Isaiah 34:8 ESV
For the LORD has a day of vengeance, a year of recompense for the cause of Zion.

The following is a summary of the seventh seal and the verse references.

NUMBER OF TRUMPET	SCRIPTURE REFERENCES	DESCRIPTION
1st Trumpet	Revelation 8:7	Hail and fire with blood: 1/3 of trees burned and all grass
2nd Trumpet	Revelation 8:8-9	Fire cast into sea: 1/3 sea becomes blood 1/3 of sea creatures die 1/3 of ships destroyed
3rd Trumpet	Revelation 8:10-11	"Star" named Wormwood: 1/3 of waters becomes bitter, many die
4th Trumpet	Revelation 8:12	Sun, moon & stars struck: 1/3 part becomes dark
5th Trumpet (1st Woe)	Revelation 9:1-11	Locusts like scorpions: torment for 5 months
6th Trumpet (2nd Woe)	Revelation 9:13-19	Horsemen from Euphrates: 1/3 part of men are slain
7th Trumpet (3rd Woe)	Revelation 15:1, 6-7; 16:1	Seven last plagues (bowls): wrath of God
1st Bowl	Revelation 16:2	Sores on those who have mark of beast
2nd Bowl	Revelation 16:3	Sea becomes blood: every living soul in sea dies
3rd Bowl	Revelation 16:4-7	Rivers and fountains become blood
4th Bowl	Revelation 16:8-9	Sun scorches with great heat and fire
5th Bowl	Revelation 16:10-11	Darkness and pain in kingdom of beast
6th Bowl	Revelation 16:12-16	Euphrates dried up: the way of the kings of the east prepared
7th Bowl	Revelation 16:17-21	Great earthquake and hail: Babylon split in three parts

Many of the parts of the seven trumpets are reminiscent of the plagues that happened in Egypt during the time of Moses. One particularly vivid judgment is the fifth trumpet or first woe. It is led by a fallen angel called "Abaddon" whose name means destruction. Right before this "woe," one-third of the light of the sun, moon and stars becomes dark. And then out of the abyss a great number of demons are released for the first of two demonic invasions. The

95

abyss, also called the bottomless pit, is a place of confinement where some demons who caused the flood were sent (2 Peter 2:4). It is also the prison where Satan and his demons will be bound for a thousand years. These demons look like locusts with scorpion tails and they torment men for five months.

Revelation 9:3-11 ESV
Then from the smoke came locusts on the earth, and they were given power like the power of scorpions of the earth.
They were told not to harm the grass of the earth or any green plant or any tree, but only those people who do not have the seal of God on their foreheads.
They were allowed to torment them for five months, but not to kill them, and their torment was like the torment of a scorpion when it stings someone.
And in those days people will seek death and will not find it. They will long to die, but death will flee from them.
In appearance the locusts were like horses prepared for battle: on their heads were what looked like crowns of gold; their faces were like human faces,
their hair like women's hair, and their teeth like lions' teeth;
they had breastplates like breastplates of iron, and the noise of their wings was like the noise of many chariots with horses rushing into battle.
They have tails and stings like scorpions, and their power to hurt people for five months is in their tails.
They have as king over them the angel of the bottomless pit. His name in Hebrew is Abaddon, and in Greek he is called Apollyon.

The sixth trumpet and second woe judgment begins with four fallen angels who are bound at the Euphrates River who are released to begin the second demonic invasion. The number of demons is given as 200 million. This section must not be pulled out of context and be interpreted as an army of the "kings of the east," especially not in reference to China. These are demons and are not human beings.

Revelation 9:15-19 ESV
So the four angels, who had been prepared for the hour, the day, the month, and the year, were released to kill a third of mankind. The number of mounted troops was twice ten thousand times ten thousand; I heard their number.
And this is how I saw the horses in my vision and those who rode them: they wore breastplates the color of fire and of sapphire and of sulfur, and the heads of the horses were like lions' heads, and fire and smoke and sulfur came out of their mouths.
By these three plagues a third of mankind was killed, by the fire and smoke and sulfur coming out of their mouths.
For the power of the horses is in their mouths and in their tails, for their tails are like serpents with heads, and by means of them they wound.

The result of this judgment is that one-third of the people of the earth are killed. Joel 2 also describes this devastation as a blazing fire with the appearance of the demons as war horses.

The wrath of God is the seventh seal in the book of Revelation

Joel 2:3-9 NET
Like fire they devour everything in their path; a flame blazes behind them. The land looks like the Garden of Eden before them, but behind them there is only a desolate wilderness– for nothing escapes them!
They look like horses; they charge ahead like war horses.
They sound like chariots rumbling over mountain tops, like the crackling of blazing fire consuming stubble, like the noise of a mighty army being drawn up for battle.

*People writhe in fear when they see them. All of their faces turn
pale with fright.*

*They charge like warriors; they scale walls like soldiers. Each one
proceeds on his course; they do not alter their path.*

*They do not jostle one another; each of them marches straight
ahead. They burst through the city defenses and do not break ranks.
They rush into the city; they scale its walls. They climb up into the
houses; they go in through the windows like a thief.*

Even with all these judgments, people refuse to repent.

Revelation 9:20-21 NET
*The rest of humanity, who had not been killed by these plagues, did
not repent of the works of their hands, so that they did not stop
worshiping demons and idols made of gold, silver, bronze, stone,
and wood– idols that cannot see or hear or walk about.*
*Furthermore, they did not repent of their murders, of their magic
spells, of their sexual immorality, or of their stealing.*

The last trumpet is sounded and includes seven "vials" or "bowls."
These bowls are filled with plagues or injuries especially targeting
the kingdom of the beast. The bowls complete the wrath of God.

Revelation 15:1, 6-7 APNT
*And I saw another sign in heaven, great and marvelous, angels
who had the seven last injuries, for in them the fury of God is completed.*
*And the seven angels came out from the temple, who had the seven
injuries, being clothed with pure and shining linen cloth and
girded on their breasts [with] a girdle of gold.*
*And one of the four living creatures gave to the seven angels seven
bowls filled with the fury of God, who is alive forever and ever.
Amen.*

THE VENGEANCE AND WRATH OF GOD

In the last bowl, the city of Babylon is destroyed by an earthquake and hail. Can you imagine the impact of hundred-pound hailstones? The effect of the earthquake is global and even the islands "flee away." The beast (Antichrist) has already gone out to gather the kings and captains of the earth together in the valley of Armageddon to fight the last battle. His destruction is after the coming of Christ with the saints.

Revelation 16:17-21 ESV
The seventh angel poured out his bowl into the air, and a loud
voice came out of the temple, from the throne, saying, "It is done!"
And there were flashes of lightning, rumblings, peals of thunder,
and a great earthquake such as there had never been since man
was on the earth, so great was that earthquake.
The great city was split into three parts, and the cities of the na-
tions fell, and God remembered Babylon the great, to make her
drain the cup of the wine of the fury of his wrath.
And every island fled away, and no mountains were to be found.
And great hailstones, about one hundred pounds each, fell from
heaven on people; and they cursed God for the plague of the hail,
because the plague was so severe.

Babylon is mentioned as being completely destroyed, never to be occupied again.

Isaiah 13:19-22 ESV
And Babylon, the glory of kingdoms, the splendor and pomp of the
Chaldeans, will be like Sodom and Gomorrah when God over-
threw them.
It will never be inhabited or lived in for all generations; no Arab
will pitch his tent there; no shepherds will make their flocks lie
down there.

*But wild animals will lie down there, and their houses will be full
of howling creatures; there ostriches will dwell, and there wild
goats will dance.*
*Hyenas will cry in its towers, and jackals in the pleasant palaces;
its time is close at hand and its days will not be prolonged.*

Revelation 18 further describes the demise of the capital of the
Antichrist with great detail.

Revelation 18:8-24 APNT
*Because of this, in one day injuries will come on her, death and
sorrow and famine, and she will be burned by fire, because the
LORD [is] mighty who has judged her.*
*And the kings of the earth will cry and wail over her, those who
fornicated with her and were arrogant, when they see the smoke of
her burning,*
*while standing away from [her] out of fear of her torment. And
they will say, 'Woe, woe, woe, [to] the great city, Babylon, the
powerful city, because in one hour your judgment has come!'*
*And the businessmen of the earth will cry and will mourn over her
and there is no one who will buy their merchandise any more,*
*the merchandise of gold and of silver and of precious stones and of
pearls and of fine linen and of purple clothing and silk of scarlet
and every aromatic wood and every vessel of ivory and every
vessel of precious wood and brass and iron and marble
and cinnamon and perfumes and myrrh and incense and wine and
oil and fine flour and sheep and horses and chariots and the
bodies and souls of men.*
*And your fruit, the desire of your soul, has gone away from you
and everything luxurious and celebrated has gone away from you
and you will not see them any more,*
*nor find them. The businessmen of these [things], who were made
rich by her, will stand away from [her] out of fear of her torment,
crying and wailing*

and saying, 'Woe, woe, [to] the great city that was clothed with fine linen and purple and scarlet [clothes] that were gilded with gold and precious stones and pearls,

because in one hour wealth like this is laid waste!' And all the masters of ships and all those traveling to places in ships and the sailors and all those who do business by sea stood a distance away.

And they cried over it as they were watching the smoke of its burning and saying, 'What [city] is like the great city?'

And they threw dust on their heads and cried out, crying and wailing and saying, 'Woe, woe, [to] the great city, in which those who had ship[s] in the sea became rich from her greatness, for in one hour she is devastated!'

Exult over her, [oh] heaven and holy [ones] and apostles and prophets, because God has judged your judgment on her."

And one of the mighty angels took a huge stone like a millstone and threw [it] into the sea and said, "So with violence Babylon, the great city, will be thrown down and you will not find [it] any more.

And the sound of the harp and of the shofar and of all kinds of music and trumpeters will not be heard in you any more.

And the light of the lamp will not be seen in you any more and the voice of the bridegroom and the voice of the bride will not be heard in you any more, because your merchants were the great [ones] of the earth, because you seduced all the nations with your enchantments,

and the blood of the prophets and the holy [ones] who were killed on the earth was found in her."

As the last of the seven bowls is being accomplished, the Antichrist and his captains and kings are gathering in the valley of Megiddo. Christ is coming soon to finish "treading the winepress of the fury of the wrath of God Almighty!" (Revelation 19:15)

CHAPTER 9 ⊕ THE DAY OF GOD ALMIGHTY

The sixth bowl judgment dries up the river Euphrates to prepare the way for the kings from the east. Then the beast (with the help of demonic spirits) gathers all the great kings and captains and mighty men to fight a battle which is called the great day of God the Almighty. The place is called Armageddon. How does this battle unfold and where is Armageddon?

Revelation 16:12-16 ESV
The sixth angel poured out his bowl on the great river Euphrates, and its water was dried up, to prepare the way for the kings from the east.
And I saw, coming out of the mouth of the dragon and out of the mouth of the beast and out of the mouth of the false prophet, three unclean spirits like frogs.
For they are demonic spirits, performing signs, who go abroad to the kings of the whole world, to assemble them for battle on the great day of God the Almighty.
("Behold, I am coming like a thief! Blessed is the one who stays awake, keeping his garments on, that he may not go about naked and be seen exposed!")
And they assembled them at the place that in Hebrew is called Armageddon.

The most common understanding of the word Armageddon is "mountain of Megiddo" and refers to the area of the city of Megiddo in northern Israel. Megiddo was the scene of a number of battles in the Old Testament. These battles, with Barak and Gideon, and also Saul and Josiah, were fought in the valley that is spread out in front of the city of Megiddo and below Mount Carmel. Megiddo is actually a city that is on a slight rise before a large valley. There are many explanations of what the term Armageddon means, but the major problem is that there is no mountain called Megiddo. The Aramaic Peshitta text says simply "Megiddo," which solves some of the argument.

The valley of Megiddo is relatively small to be the center of a battle with "all the kings of the whole world." So what does Megiddo mean? The best explanation I offer is to understand it being not as a place, but as a generic noun from the verb root in Hebrew. The root idea of *gadad* (Strong's #1413) is "to cut" and also "to gather in troops or bands."[38] The "on" at the end of Armageddon means "the place of" in Hebrew. Megiddo is the name of an ancient city, but with the letter *mem* in front of the verb *gadad*, it turns the verb into a noun. Then it could mean "the place of the gathering of troops."

An additional explanation is that the word for battle in Revelation 16 can mean "war" and not just one battle. Several very prominent scholars have called this time a "campaign" instead of just one battle.[39] Multiple groups of people are involved: kings of the whole world, kings from the east, Gog and Magog, and of course the Antichrist. The best label to call this end time war is "The Day of God Almighty" as it is called in Revelation.

Putting together the book of Revelation with the Prophets, there are four centers and places of the gathering of troops in this end time war with four separate fronts:

---

[38] Brown, Francis, *The New Brown Driver Briggs Gesenius Hebrew and English Lexicon*, p. 151.
[39] Pentecost, Dwight. *Things to Come*, pp.343-347.

THE DAY OF GOD ALMIGHTY

Locations	Primary Participants	Scriptures
1. Along the Euphrates River	Kings of the East	Revelation 16:12 Isaiah 49:12
2. Babylon	From north country	Jeremiah 46:10; 50:9 Jeremiah 51:27-58
3. Jerusalem	Antichrist and his troops	Daniel 11:45 Zechariah 12-14
4. East of Dead Sea	Coalition of Gog and Magog	Ezekiel 38-39

The first gathering of troops is described only in Revelation 16 and says that a highway for the kings of the east is enabled because of the drying up of the Euphrates River. Several Old Testament passages may refer to this army of the kings of the east. Daniel 11 says that the Antichrist is concerned about what he hears from the east and goes out to fight against them.

Daniel 11:44 ESV
But news from the east and the north shall alarm him, and he shall go out with great fury to destroy and devote many to destruction.

The Euphrates River has always been the boundary between the countries surrounding Israel and the nations to the Far East. There is a passage in Isaiah which may refer to the farthest reaches of the east which the King James Version calls Sinim. This could be China but it also could be an alliance of several countries from the east.

Isaiah 49:12 KJV
Behold, these shall come from far: and, lo, these from the north and from the west; and these from the land of Sinim.

Smith's Bible Dictionary gives the common understanding of Sinim as "a people noticed in Isaiah 49:12, as living at the extremity of the

104

known world. They may be identified with the classical *Sinae*, the inhabitants of the southern part of China."[40]

Rather than speculate what exactly will happen in this first stage, this is what we know. There are kings from the east which gather somewhere near the Euphrates River and are part of the day of the Lord battles. There is no description of an actual battle, only that they are gathered together for battle and that the Lord God of hosts will interfere and conquer them.

Jeremiah 46:10 ESV
That day is the day of the Lord GOD of hosts, a day of vengeance, to avenge himself on his foes. The sword shall devour and be sated and drink its fill of their blood. For the Lord GOD of hosts holds a sacrifice in the north country by the river Euphrates.

The second gathering of troops is with people from the north and is directed against the capital city of the Antichrist, Babylon. We have seen in the previous chapter that Babylon is destroyed by an earthquake as part of the last

Armageddon has four stages and fronts and is called the day of God Almighty

bowl judgment. It is also clear from the Old Testament that several specific nations will be involved in the destruction of Babylon. These verses were already partially fulfilled when Babylonia was conquered by the Medes and Persians, but this end time scene will crush Babylon completely.

Jeremiah 50:9 ESV
For behold, I am stirring up and bringing against Babylon a gathering of great nations, from the north country. And they shall

---

[40] Smith, William. *A Dictionary of the Bible,* p. 637.

array themselves against her. From there she shall be taken. Their arrows are like a skilled warrior who does not return empty-handed.

Nations from the areas of eastern Turkey and northern Iran, Armenia and Asia Minor will all be involved. This is the former empire of the Medes and Persians.

Jeremiah 51:27-33 ESV
Set up a standard on the earth; blow the trumpet among the nations; prepare the nations for war against her; summon against her the kingdoms, Ararat, Minni, and Ashkenaz; appoint a marshal against her; bring up horses like bristling locusts.
Prepare the nations for war against her, the kings of the Medes, with their governors and deputies, and every land under their dominion.
The land trembles and writhes in pain, for the LORD's purposes against Babylon stand, to make the land of Babylon a desolation, without inhabitant.
The warriors of Babylon have ceased fighting; they remain in their strongholds; their strength has failed; they have become women; her dwellings are on fire; her bars are broken.
One runner runs to meet another, and one messenger to meet another, to tell the king of Babylon that his city is taken on every side;
the fords have been seized, the marshes are burned with fire, and the soldiers are in panic.
For thus says the LORD of hosts, the God of Israel: The daughter of Babylon is like a threshing floor at the time when it is trodden; yet a little while and the time of her harvest will come."

Babylon will be completely punished for her idolatry and what was done to Israel. There are many prophecies against Babylon in the scriptures. Jeremiah explains clearly that it is the LORD who is punishing Babylon.

Jeremiah 51:52-58 NET
Yes, but the time will certainly come," says the LORD, "when I
will punish her idols. Throughout her land the mortally wounded
will groan.
Even if Babylon climbs high into the sky and fortifies her elevated
stronghold, I will send destroyers against her," says the LORD.
Cries of anguish will come from Babylon, the sound of great
destruction from the land of the Babylonians.
For the LORD is ready to destroy Babylon, and put an end to her
loud noise. Their waves will roar like turbulent waters. They will
make a deafening noise.
For a destroyer is attacking Babylon. Her warriors will be
captured; their bows will be broken. For the LORD is a God who
punishes; he pays back in full.
"I will make her officials and wise men drunk, along with her
governors, leaders, and warriors. They will fall asleep forever and
never wake up," says the King whose name is the LORD who rules
over all.
This is what the LORD who rules over all says, "Babylon's thick
wall will be completely demolished. Her high gates will be set on
fire. The peoples strive for what does not satisfy. The nations grow
weary trying to get what will be destroyed."

The third place of the gathering of troops is focused against Jerusalem and involves the Antichrist's army. This is where the valley of Megiddo is possibly the staging area for attacks against Jerusalem.

THE DAY OF GOD ALMIGHTY

Daniel 11:45 KJV
And he shall plant the tabernacles of his palace between the seas
in the glorious holy mountain; yet he shall come to his end, and
none shall help him.

The "tabernacles of his palace" are the Antichrist's royal tents. He sets up camp somewhere between the Mediterranean Sea and the Dead Sea. Zechariah has the most complete description of this part of the war in chapters 12-14.

Zechariah 12:2-4 TNK
Behold, I will make Jerusalem a bowl of reeling for the peoples all
around. Judah shall be caught up in the siege upon Jerusalem,
when all the nations of the earth gather against her. In that day, I
will make Jerusalem a stone for all the peoples to lift; all who lift it
shall injure themselves.
In that day– declares the LORD– I will strike every horse with
panic and its rider with madness. But I will watch over the House
of Judah while I strike every horse of the peoples with blindness.

God fights against the Antichrist's army but this part of the campaign is not finished until Christ returns. Two thirds of the people perish and there is much devastation.

Zechariah 13:8-9 TNK
Throughout the land– declares the LORD– Two-thirds shall per-
ish, shall die, And one-third of it shall survive.
That third I will put into the fire, And I will smelt them as one
smelts silver And test them as one tests gold. They will invoke Me
by name, And I will respond to them. I will declare, "You are My
people," And they will declare, "The LORD is our God!"

There is much violation and plundering in the city and people are taken captive. Again, this is part of the "day of the LORD."

THE DAY OF GOD ALMIGHTY

Zechariah 14:1-3 TNK
Lo, a day of the LORD is coming when your spoil shall be divided
in your very midst!
For I will gather all the nations to Jerusalem for war: The city
shall be captured, the houses plundered, and the women violated;
and a part of the city shall go into exile. But the rest of the popula-
tion shall not be uprooted from the city.
Then the LORD will come forth and make war on those nations as
He is wont to make war on a day of battle.

The fourth front of the war occurs south of Jerusalem in the
mountains east of the Dead Sea. There is a remnant of the Jews who
have fled to the wilderness where they have been cared for during
the tribulation. Some say they flee to Petra, but there are some
problems with that theory because of the remoteness of access to the
city and the lack of water there. It is at least somewhere in that
general location. There is a prophecy against Edom (the nation from
the lineage of Esau) that shows how Edom will be a staging ground
for the final victory of Jesus Christ at his return. This prophecy
mentions a city called Bozrah, which means "sheepfold" in Hebrew.
This town is about 80 miles southeast of Jerusalem in the land of
Edom, or modern-day Jordan. What happens on this day of "great
slaughter" is described in Isaiah.

Isaiah 34:1-7 ESV
Draw near, O nations, to hear, and give attention, O peoples! Let
the earth hear, and all that fills it; the world, and all that comes
from it.
For the LORD is enraged against all the nations, and furious
against all their host; he has devoted them to destruction, has
given them over for slaughter.
Their slain shall be cast out, and the stench of their corpses shall
rise; the mountains shall flow with their blood.

THE DAY OF GOD ALMIGHTY

*All the host of heaven shall rot away, and the skies roll up like a
scroll. All their host shall fall, as leaves fall from the vine, like
leaves falling from the fig tree.
For my sword has drunk its fill in the heavens; behold, it descends
for judgment upon Edom, upon the people I have devoted to destruction.
The LORD has a sword; it is sated with blood; it is gorged with
fat, with the blood of lambs and goats, with the fat of the kidneys of
rams. For the LORD has a sacrifice in Bozrah, a great slaughter
in the land of Edom.*

Bozrah, sometimes spelled Botzrah or Botsra, was the capital city
of Edom where Esau lived. How exactly this city will be involved
in the day of God Almighty is yet to be seen in how the prophecies
will be fulfilled. But it will definitely be involved. This portion of
the war will be like the time when God rained down fire and brimstone on Sodom and Gomorrah.

*Jeremiah 49:13-18 NASB
"For I have sworn by Myself," declares the LORD, "that Bozrah
will become an object of horror, a reproach, a ruin and a curse;
and all its cities will become perpetual ruins."
I have heard a message from the LORD, And an envoy is sent
among the nations, saying, "Gather yourselves together and come
against her, And rise up for battle!"
"For behold, I have made you small among the nations, Despised
among men.
"As for the terror of you, The arrogance of your heart has deceived you, O you who live in the clefts of the rock, Who occupy
the height of the hill. Though you make your nest as high as an ea-
gle's, I will bring you down from there," declares the LORD.
"And Edom will become an object of horror; everyone who passes
by it will be horrified and will hiss at all its wounds.*

THE DAY OF GOD ALMIGHTY

*"Like the overthrow of Sodom and Gomorrah with its neighbors,"
says the LORD, "no one will live there, nor will a son of man re-
side in it."*

Edom is prominently shamed in the "day of vengeance" also. It is
apparent that God is the one fighting the battle.

Isaiah 63:1-6 ESV
*Who is this who comes from Edom, in crimsoned garments from
Bozrah, he who is splendid in his apparel, marching in the greatness of his strength? "It is I, speaking in righteousness, mighty to
save."*
*Why is your apparel red, and your garments like his who treads in
the winepress?*
*"I have trodden the winepress alone, and from the peoples no one
was with me; I trod them in my anger and trampled them in my
wrath; their lifeblood spattered on my garments, and stained all
my apparel.*
*For the day of vengeance was in my heart, and my year of redemp-
tion had come.*
*I looked, but there was no one to help; I was appalled, but there
was no one to uphold; so my own arm brought me salvation, and
my wrath upheld me.*
*I trampled down the peoples in my anger; I made them drunk in my
wrath, and I poured out their lifeblood on the earth."*

Amos also describes the overthrow of Bozrah.

Amos 1:11-12 NASB
*Thus says the LORD, "For three transgressions of Edom and for
four I will not revoke its punishment, Because he pursued his
brother with the sword, While he stifled his compassion; His anger
also tore continually, And he maintained his fury forever.*

THE DAY OF GOD ALMIGHTY

"So I will send fire upon Teman, And it will consume the citadels of Bozrah."

It is amazing how many prophecies there are about the center of Bozrah! The "great day of God Almighty" is about to be concluded.

Who is involved in this part of the war? Ezekiel chapters 38 and 39 provide some very interesting descriptions. They pertain to a gathering of nations called Gog and Magog. Part of the description, especially in chapter 38, cannot be the same as this event at the end times, so either it is a previous war before the Antichrist is in power or it has been fulfilled before in history. But part of it is vividly linked with the descriptions of Christ treading the winepress of the wrath of God which is this last stage of the war.

The nations described in Ezekiel 38:5-6 are Persia (modern Iran), Cush (Ethiopia), Phut (northern Africa), Gomer (eastern Turkey), Beth Togarmah (central Asia) and Rosh, Gog, Magog, Meshack, and Tubal (all western Turkey or Asia Minor). These nations are located in the same general areas as the nations of the north who destroyed Babylon, so it is possible that they continue on from there to come up against the remnant of the Jews hiding in the wilderness. If the nations are not the same, they are another coalition from similar areas and include countries from Africa as well.

As the description in Ezekiel continues, the details of this stage of the war become evident. This part of the battle is fought by God and includes fire and brimstone and hail.

Ezekiel 38:21-23 ESV
I will summon a sword against Gog on all my mountains, declares the Lord GOD. Every man's sword will be against his brother.

112

With pestilence and bloodshed I will enter into judgment with him, and I will rain upon him and his hordes and the many peoples who are with him torrential rains and hailstones, fire and sulfur.
So I will show my greatness and my holiness and make myself known in the eyes of many nations. Then they will know that I am the LORD.

Another indication of this being the same description is that people are given to the birds of prey to eat and again there is fire in the passage. This same event is called the "great supper of God" in Revelation 19:17.

Ezekiel 39:1-6 ESV
And you, son of man, prophesy against Gog and say, Thus says the Lord GOD: Behold, I am against you, O Gog, chief prince of Meshech and Tubal.
And I will turn you about and drive you forward, and bring you up from the uttermost parts of the north, and lead you against the mountains of Israel.
Then I will strike your bow from your left hand, and will make your arrows drop out of your right hand.
You shall fall on the mountains of Israel, you and all your hordes and the peoples who are with you. I will give you to birds of prey of every sort and to the beasts of the field to be devoured.
You shall fall in the open field, for I have spoken, declares the Lord GOD.
I will send fire on Magog and on those who dwell securely in the coastlands, and they shall know that I am the LORD.

The mountains of Israel are the location of this part of the war and the carrion birds are invited.

THE DAY OF GOD ALMIGHTY

Ezekiel 39:17 KJV
And thou son of man, thus saith the Lord God; Speak unto every feathered fowl, and to every beast of the field, Assemble yourselves, and come; gather yourselves on every side to My sacrifice that I do sacrifice for you, even a great sacrifice upon the mountains of Israel, that ye may eat flesh, and drink blood.

The gathering of the troops has occurred and the places have been defended by the Lord God Almighty. The time has come for the appearance of the Messiah, the King!

CHAPTER 10 ⚜ THE COMING OF THE SON OF MAN

Events	Scriptures
Banner of the Son of Man seen in the clouds	Matthew 24:27-30 Revelation 1:7
Coming of Christ on white horse as King of kings	Revelation 19:11-16 Jude 14
The harvest of the earth	Revelation 14:14-16
Carrion birds invited to the "great supper of God," winepress of wrath	Revelation 19:17-18 Revelation 14:18-20 Ezekiel 39:17-22
Defeat of Antichrist's army in Jerusalem	Zechariah 14:12-15
Beast and false prophet cast into the lake of fire	Revelation 19:19-21

Christ is coming and will make his appearance visibly. The word for "appearing" or "appearance" in Greek is *epiphaneia*. It means something shone forth. Thayer's Greek Lexicon defines this word as "*appearing, appearance*…; often used by the Greeks of a glorious manifestation of the gods, and especially of their advent to help… of signal deeds and events betokening the presence and power of God as helper;"[41] This is now the time when Christ will shine out the power of God and bring "divine assistance."[42] The Antichrist will be slain with the "breath of his mouth" and be brought to a swift end.

---

[41] Thayer, Joseph Henry. *The New Thayer's Greek-English Lexicon*, p. 245.

[42] Bromiley, Geoffrey W. *Kittel's Theological Dictionary of the New Testament*, p. 1246.

THE COMING OF THE SON OF MAN

2 Thessalonians 2:8 NASB
And then that lawless one will be revealed whom the Lord will slay
with the breath of His mouth and bring to an end by the appear-
ance [epiphaneia] of His coming;

The breath of his mouth is a reference to a passage in Isaiah.

Isaiah 11:4 ESV
but with righteousness he shall judge the poor, and decide with
equity for the meek of the earth; and he shall strike the earth with
the rod of his mouth, and with the breath of his lips he shall kill the
wicked.

All throughout the time of the seven trumpets, it is repeatedly said
that men repented *not* of their deeds. They were lulled by the "peace
and safety" of the time. The prosperity is going to be unimaginable.
Revelation 18:9-19 describes the merchants and kings mourning because of the destruction of Babylon and the loss of all the wealth.
Most people will be oblivious to what is going on, even though the
Scriptures have foretold these things over and over. The believers
are continually exhorted to watch, for the coming of the Son of Man
will be like the days of Noah and Lot.

Luke 17:26-30 KJV
And as it was in the days of Noe, so shall it be also in the days of
the Son of man.
They did eat, they drank, they married wives, they were given in
marriage, until the day that Noe entered into the ark, and the flood
came, and destroyed them all.
Likewise also as it was in the days of Lot; they did eat, they drank,
they bought, they sold, they planted, they builded;
But the same day that Lot went out of Sodom it rained fire and
brimstone from heaven, and destroyed them all.
Even thus shall it be in the day when the Son of man is revealed.

THE COMING OF THE SON OF MAN

People will continue as though nothing unusual is going on, even though the cataclysmic events from the seven trumpets will have been happening. There will be blood in the sea, fish being killed and many earthquakes, yet people are oblivious!

Then as lightning, the Son of Man shall come! The Messiah is coming to the earth to personally rescue his people from danger. This is the climax of the movie of the Hope! When lightning splits the sky, light is seen from east to west. The sun and moon are again darkened and the "powers of heaven" are shaken. This is the third time the sun and moon are darkened.

Matthew 24:27-29 APNT
For as the lightning comes out of the east and is visible into the west, so the arrival of the Son of Man will be.
Wherever the carcass will be, there the eagles will be gathered.
And immediately after the ordeal of those days, the sun will grow dark and the moon will not shine its light and stars will fall from heaven and the powers of heaven will be shaken.

The arrival of the Son of Man means that Christ is coming to claim his kingdom as described in Daniel.

Daniel 7:13-14 NIV
"In my vision at night I looked, and there before me was one like a son of man, coming with the clouds of heaven. He approached the Ancient of Days and was led into his presence.
He was given authority, glory and sovereign power; all nations and peoples of every language worshiped him. His dominion is an everlasting dominion that will not pass away, and his kingdom is one that will never be destroyed.

The title "Son of Man," as used by Jesus in the Gospels, is an understated reference. He was a *bar'nasha,* a man like one of us, but

117

also the Christ, the Messiah, the anointed one of God. Jesus is coming back as a prophet, priest and king. As king he will be coming as a judge. That is why he called himself the Son of Man.

John 5:25-27 NIV
Very truly I tell you, a time is coming and has now come when the dead will hear the voice of the Son of God and those who hear will live.
For as the Father has life in himself, so he has granted the Son also to have life in himself.
And he has given him authority to judge because he is the Son of Man.

> *The title Son of Man is Christ's authority as the judge of all the inhabitants of the earth, past, present and future.*

Bullinger denotes the use of "Son of Man" with the definite article to differentiate it as a title and not just the simple meaning of "man." He describes it as the figure of speech, *pleonasm*:

> It is according to this Figure or Hebraism that Christ is called "the Son of Man," as *the* man, the representative man, the man who had been long promised as the seed of the woman; the man prophesied. Therefore this title used of Christ usually has reference to that aspect of His work as the appointed Judge of men (Acts 17:31). "The Son of Man" is therefore an emphatic dispensational title of Christ. It means merely "man," but with emphasis on all that the word means as used of Christ and his dominion in the earth.[43]

---

[43] Bullinger, E.W. *Figures of Speech Used in the Bible*, p. 408.

THE COMING OF THE SON OF MAN

Acts 17:30-31 ESV
The times of ignorance God overlooked, but now he commands all
people everywhere to repent,
because he has fixed a day on which he will judge the world in
righteousness by a man whom he has appointed; and of this he has
given assurance to all by raising him from the dead.

The judge is coming in the clouds with power and great glory!
During his trial in Jerusalem, Jesus was asked if he was the Messiah
and this is how he responded.

Matthew 26:63-64 ESV
But Jesus remained silent. And the high priest said to him, "I ad-
jure you by the living God, tell us if you are the Christ, the Son of
God."
Jesus said to him, "You have said so. But I tell you, from now on
you will see the Son of Man seated at the right hand of Power and
coming on the clouds of heaven."

In the Old Testament, the cloud is the symbol of God's presence in
the midst of the people. He used clouds to guard the children of
Israel in the wilderness and he will send his Son back to the earth
with majestic clouds.

Psalm 104:1-3 ESV
Bless the LORD, O my soul! O LORD my God, you are very great!
You are clothed with splendor and majesty,
covering yourself with light as with a garment, stretching out the
heavens like a tent.
He lays the beams of his chambers on the waters; he makes the
clouds his chariot; he rides on the wings of the wind;

The banner of Jesus Christ will be the first thing seen in the clouds.

THE COMING OF THE SON OF MAN

Matthew 24:30 APNT
And then the standard of the Son of Man will be seen in heaven.
And then all the tribes of the earth will mourn and they will see the
Son of Man who comes on the clouds of heaven with power and
great glory.

The Aramaic word for "sign" as in many other English translations is *nisha*. It corresponds to the Hebrew word *nissa*. This word is used in one of the Jehovah names, Jehovah Nissi, meaning the Lord my banner. The standard was used in the days of Moses as the emblem of the various tribes. When the banners were brought together from the tribes and raised, it was the call to war.

In the first chapter of Revelation, John prophesied about the Lord coming in the clouds. The coming of Christ will be a universal experience in the sense that every eye will witness the event.

Revelation 1:7 NET
Look! He is returning with the clouds, and every eye will see him,
even those who pierced him, and all the tribes on the earth will
mourn because of him. This will certainly come to pass! Amen.

All the people of the earth mourn when they see Christ on the white horse because they realize that everything that was in the prophecies is now coming to pass! "Those who pierced him" refers to Zechariah 12:10 which is the prophecy about how Jesus would be pierced on the cross. It cannot be the literal people of the first century. This is a figure of speech, emphasizing that the Judeans were originally responsible for Christ's death. Now they will be confronted with the truth of his resurrection.

Revelation 19 describes the coming of Christ in more detail and that his name is called "The Word of God."

THE COMING OF THE SON OF MAN

Revelation 19:11-13 KJV
And I saw heaven opened, and behold a white horse; and he that
sat upon him was called Faithful and True, and in righteousness
he doth judge and make war.
His eyes were as a flame of fire, and on his head were many
crowns; and he had a name written, that no man knew, but he him-
self.
And he was clothed with a vesture dipped in blood: and his name
is called The Word of God.

The next thing that people will see is the sharp sword out of his
mouth. It will be the reason that people mourn, as it describes in
Matthew 24. The title on his robe, King of kings and Lord of lords,
will be clear and prominent. John Wesley comments about this,
"That is, on the part of his vesture which is upon his thigh. A name
written– It was usual of old, for great personages in the eastern countries, to have magnificent titles affixed to their garments."[44] It is also
interesting to note that the Peshitta says "their mouths" in the plural,
so perhaps all the members of the heavenly army will have swords
coming out of their mouths. In either case, it is not certain whether
these swords are literal or figurative.

Revelation 19:14-16 APNT
And the armies in heaven were following him on white horses and
were clothed with fine linen, white and pure.
And from their mouth[s] a sharp sword came out, with which to
kill the nations. And he will rule them with a rod of iron and he
will tread the winepress of the anger of God Almighty.
And he had a name written on his garments, on his thighs, "King
of kings and Lord of lords."

---

[44] Wesley, John, *Notes on the Bible*, Revelation 19:16.

THE COMING OF THE SON OF MAN

What we do know is that this is the fulfillment of the prophecy of Enoch, the seventh man from Adam, as it says in Jude 14: "Behold, the Lord cometh with ten thousands of His saints." We will be with him and it will be time to make war! He is coming in the clouds as the Son of Man to reap the earth with his sharp sickle. There is vivid imagery associated with the Lord's return to harvest the earth.

Revelation 14:14-16 ESV
Then I looked, and behold, a white cloud, and seated on the cloud one like a son of man, with a golden crown on his head, and a sharp sickle in his hand.
And another angel came out of the temple, calling with a loud voice to him who sat on the cloud, "Put in your sickle, and reap, for the hour to reap has come, for the harvest of the earth is fully ripe."
So he who sat on the cloud swung his sickle across the earth, and the earth was reaped.

THE GREAT SUPPER OF GOD

The first place that Jesus Christ returns is to the wilderness of Edom to rescue the Jews from the attacks of the nations. He has not actually touched the earth yet. But he carries out treading the winepress of the wrath of God.

Revelation 19:17-19 APNT
And I saw another angel standing in the sun and he cried out with a loud voice and said to the bird[s] that fly in the middle of heaven, "Come, gather together for the great supper of God, that you may eat the flesh of the kings and the flesh of the rulers of thousands and the flesh of the powerful [ones] and the flesh of the horses and of those who sit on them and the flesh of the free [men] and of the servants and of the small and of the great."

THE COMING OF THE SON OF MAN

And I saw the creature and his hosts and the kings of the earth and their soldiers gathering to wage war with him who sits on the stallion and with his armies.

This is the "great supper of God" and Jesus Christ finishes the war with the sharp sword out of his mouth and invites the carrion birds to feast on the flesh. An angel thrusts his sickle into the earth and gathers the vine of the earth and casts it into the great winepress of the wrath of God. This is described in the continuation of the passage in Revelation 14.

Revelation 14:18-20 NASB
And another angel, the one who has power over fire, came out from the altar; and he called with a loud voice to him who had the sharp sickle, saying, "Put in your sharp sickle, and gather the clusters from the vine of the earth, because her grapes are ripe."
And the angel swung his sickle to the earth, and gathered the clusters from the vine of the earth, and threw them into the great wine press of the wrath of God.
And the wine press was trodden outside the city, and blood came out from the wine press, up to the horses' bridles, for a distance of two hundred miles.

The winepress and the harvest are both descriptions of the end of the wrath of God

In this prophecy, wine symbolizes the bloodshed which the wicked have caused and when it is said that Jesus Christ treads the winepress of God, it means he will squeeze the lifeblood from his enemies down to the last drop. The wicked will be crushed like grapes and utterly destroyed. The blood will be as deep as up to the "horses' bridles." The blood is running for a distance of over two hundred miles.

THE COMING OF THE SON OF MAN

The carrion birds swoop in to feast on the bodies of all of the enemies of Israel. Ezekiel has a detailed description of this "great supper" for the birds.

Ezekiel 39:17-22 KJV
And, thou son of man, thus saith the Lord GOD; Speak unto every feathered fowl, and to every beast of the field, Assemble yourselves, and come; gather yourselves on every side to my sacrifice that I do sacrifice for you, even a great sacrifice upon the mountains of Israel, that ye may eat flesh, and drink blood.
Ye shall eat the flesh of the mighty, and drink the blood of the princes of the earth, of rams, of lambs, and of goats, of bullocks, all of them fatlings of Bashan.
And ye shall eat fat till ye be full, and drink blood till ye be drunken, of my sacrifice which I have sacrificed for you.
Thus ye shall be filled at my table with horses and chariots, with mighty men, and with all men of war, saith the Lord GOD.
And I will set my glory among the heathen, and all the heathen shall see my judgment that I have executed, and my hand that I have laid upon them.
So the house of Israel shall know that I am the LORD their God from that day and forward.

Now Christ turns toward Jerusalem to confront the Antichrist's army there. There is a description in Zechariah of what happens in this last part of the great conflict with the Antichrist.

Zechariah 14:12-15 NASB
Now this will be the plague with which the LORD will strike all the peoples who have gone to war against Jerusalem; their flesh will rot while they stand on their feet, and their eyes will rot in their sockets, and their tongue will rot in their mouth.

124

THE COMING OF THE SON OF MAN

And it will come about in that day that a great panic from the LORD will fall on them; and they will seize one another's hand, and the hand of one will be lifted against the hand of another. And Judah also will fight at Jerusalem; and the wealth of all the surrounding nations will be gathered, gold and silver and garments in great abundance.
So also like this plague, will be the plague on the horse, the mule, the camel, the donkey, and all the cattle that will be in those camps.

Jesus Christ defeats the Antichrist (beast) and all his armies. He either slays them all with a plague and the sword or they kill each other! Several other verses describe the demise of the Antichrist (the Assyrian). It is an especially dramatic picture that Jesus Christ will destroy him and all the wicked ones with the sword coming out of his mouth. He will "crush" or "break in pieces" the wicked one.

Habakkuk 3:13 NET
You march out to deliver your people, to deliver your special servant. You strike the leader of the wicked nation, laying him open from the lower body to the neck.

Isaiah 14:25 NIV
I will crush the Assyrian in my land; on my mountains I will trample him down. His yoke will be taken from my people, and his burden removed from their shoulders.

THE LAKE OF FIRE

Then immediately the beast and the false prophet are thrown in the lake of fire. This is the first mention of the lake of fire in Revelation.

Revelation 19:19-21 KJV
And I saw the beast, and the kings of the earth, and their armies, gathered together to make war against him that sat on the horse, and against his army.
And the beast was taken, and with him the false prophet that wrought miracles before him, with which he deceived them that had received the mark of the beast, and them that worshipped his image. These both were cast alive into a lake of fire burning with brimstone.
And the remnant were slain with the sword of him that sat upon the horse, which sword proceeded out of his mouth: and all the fowls were filled with their flesh.

The lake of fire is said to be burning with brimstone, or sulphur. There are only four times the phrase "lake of fire" is used in Revelation. But this place is also described in the Old Testament and is called Tophet or Topheth.

Isaiah 30:33 NASB
For Topheth has long been ready, Indeed, it has been prepared for the king. He has made it deep and large, A pyre of fire with plenty of wood; The breath of the LORD, like a torrent of brimstone, sets it afire.

Tophet was a place in the valley of Hinnom (Gehenna) in southeast Jerusalem that perhaps was a garden originally, but during the time of Solomon it became a place of offering sacrifices to Baal and Molech. Later idolatrous kings made their children "pass through the fire" in this valley "and the fiendish custom of infant sacrifice to the fire-gods seems to have been kept up in Tophet."[45] Later, good kings tore down the altars and high places and made it a garbage dump that was continually on fire. This burning of the garbage in Gehenna

---

[45] Smith, William. *A Dictionary of the Bible*, p. 250.

is the lake of fire and is also translated as "hell." Gehenna or hell is not a place in the deepest part of the earth where wicked people go after they die, but according to the book of Revelation it is a place of fire where the wicked will be punished.

The first people to go in the lake of fire are the Antichrist and the false prophet. There will be more as Christ begins the judgments. This is the description of the coming of the Son of Man. Now Jesus Christ begins to put things back together and paves the way for the start of the Millennial Reign. It's time for Christ to do the judging!

CHAPTER 11 ⬥ THE KINGDOM ESTABLISHED

Events	Scriptures
Jesus' feet land on Mount of Olives and mountain splits in two	Zechariah 14:4
Gathering of the elect	Matthew 24:31
	Mark 13:27-37
	Luke 17:25-36
	Deuteronomy 30:3-5
	Ezekiel 34:12-13
	Isaiah 27:12-13
144,000 with Christ on Mount Zion	Revelation 14:1-5
Satan is bound	Revelation 20:1-3
Judgment of the Gentiles	Joel 3:1-2, 14
	Matthew 25:31-46
Resurrection of the Just	Revelation 20:4
	Isaiah 26:19
	Ezekiel 37:1-14
	Joel 2:28-29
Marriage Supper of the Lamb	Revelation 19:7
	John 14:1-3
	Revelation 21:9-12

The actual place of Christ's return to the earth will be to the Mount of Olives. After the ascension, the two men in white apparel said to the apostles, "this same Jesus, which is taken up from you into heaven, shall so come in like manner as ye have seen Him go into heaven" (Acts 1:11). Zechariah says that the Mount of Olives will be split in two as soon as his feet touch the earth.

Zechariah 14:4 NET
On that day his feet will stand on the Mount of Olives which lies to the east of Jerusalem, and the Mount of Olives will be split in half from east to west, leaving a great valley. Half the mountain will move northward and the other half southward.

This splitting of the mountain causes two things: 1) water flows out to irrigate the land west to the Mediterranean Sea and east to the Dead Sea and 2) the valley next to Jerusalem is enlarged so that it can be the place of the judgment of the nations. Today it is known geologically that there is a fault line underneath the mount of Olives and also a huge underground water source.[46] That makes this prophecy possible!

GATHERING OF THE ELECT

With the coming of Christ Jesus, the reign of the king from heaven begins. His kingdom is going to be established on earth. The first thing that Christ does after his return is to send his angels to gather together all those alive of Israel to Mount Zion. This gathering together is recorded in Matthew 24:31-51, Mark 13:27-37, and Luke 17:34-37.

Matthew 24:31 NET
And he will send his angels with a loud trumpet blast, and they will gather his elect from the four winds, from one end of heaven to the other.

This gathering together is completely different from the gathering together of the Church of the Body. This gathering is described in Deuteronomy and is clear that it is about Israel.

Deuteronomy 30:3-5 NLT
then the LORD your God will restore your fortunes. He will have mercy on you and gather you back from all the nations where he has scattered you.
Even though you are banished to the ends of the earth, the LORD your God will gather you from there and bring you back again.

---

[46] www.abbaswatchman.com: The Dead Sea Prophecy

The LORD your God will return you to the land that belonged to your ancestors, and you will possess that land again. Then he will make you even more prosperous and numerous than your ancestors!

The use of the phrases "outmost parts of heaven" (KJV), "from the four winds," and "from the uttermost part of the earth to the uttermost part of heaven" (Mark 13:27) lead one to believe that this gathering could be the same as the first resurrection with both the alive and the dead of Israel. However, there are several discrepancies to that conclusion. First of all, the record in Revelation 20 of the resurrection says that there are thrones in the vision of the first resurrection. Secondly, since not all Israel are dead, then it is not technically a resurrection.

There are several figures of speech used in Matthew 24:31 that will clarify the topic. First of all, "from the four winds" is a *metonymy*. The four winds are attributed to the four quarters of the earth. "From one end of heaven..." is also a *metonymy*, where the appearance stands for the thing itself. It means, "from where the earth seems to touch the heaven."[47] The use of these figures gives emphasis to the extent to which Israel has been scattered and how great it is that they are being gathered together. Certainly, part of the people who are being gathered are those who had fled from Jerusalem after the abomination of desolation was set up and had been hidden in the wilderness. But there will also be others who remained alive through the great tribulation.

Ezekiel 34 describes the gathering as a shepherd seeking out his flock.

---

[47] Bullinger, *Figures of Speech Used in the Bible*, p. 598.

Ezekiel 34:12-13 NLT
I will be like a shepherd looking for his scattered flock. I will find
my sheep and rescue them from all the places where they were
scattered on that dark and cloudy day.
I will bring them back home to their own land of Israel from
among the peoples and nations. I will feed them on the mountains
of Israel and by the rivers and in all the places where people live.

Isaiah also describes the gathering as threshing out the grain, glean-
ing it one by one.

Isaiah 27:12-13 ESV
In that day from the river Euphrates to the Brook of Egypt the
LORD will thresh out the grain, and you will be gleaned one by
one, O people of Israel.
And in that day a great trumpet will be blown, and those who were
lost in the land of Assyria and those who were driven out to the
land of Egypt will come and worship the LORD on the holy moun-
tain at Jerusalem.

Who are the ones to be gathered together? The answer lies in the
records in Matthew 24:40-41 and Luke 17:34-36. They can be
studied to see how the "two in the field" and the "one taken" means
to be taken to one's side in blessing. The major point these records
reveal is that there will be people alive after the end of the
tribulation. Those left will have endured until Christ's coming. The
Gospels call them "the elect" or "chosen ones." From a study of the
words for "elect," and "to choose," it is interesting to note that the
verb to choose, *eklegomai*, is defined as "to pick out for one's self,
choose out, from preference, favour or love" and "to lay out
together, to pick out for one's self, choose out, select, not implying
the rejection of that which is not chosen, but like the choosing of
Levi from the twelve tribes; to choose out, with the accessory idea

of kindness, favour, love."[48] The elect, therefore, are a people of Israel, singled out for special favor and love.

One consideration fitting this description is the 144,000 of Israel who were sealed before the tribulation began. They may not be the only ones of Israel left after the tribulation, but they are absolutely part of all who are gathered. The sealing allowed them to endure the persecution and tribulation and Revelation 14:1-5 explains why they should be called elect and be so favored.

Revelation 14:1 shows that these 144,000 are gathered to Mount Zion. There they stand with the Lamb. The vision in this section shows that they are gathered together, stand with Christ on Mount Zion, and then are redeemed, being the "firstfruits unto God and to the Lamb" (verse 4). The place of the vision changes to the throne of God with the four living creatures and the elders. The redeemed ones proceed to sing a new song before the throne.

The study of the word firstfruits, *aparche*, shows that there are various ways it is used. It is used of the saints who have the firstfruits of the spirit (Romans 8:23), of Christ as the firstfruits of them that slept (1 Corinthians 15:20, 23), of Epaenetus and the house of Stephanos as the firstfruits of Achaia (Romans 16:5, 1 Corinthians 16:15), and of another group of believers as a "kind of firstfruits" (James 1:18). Israel as a nation is also called "firstfruit" in Romans 11:16.

To call the 144,000 the firstfruits shows that they are the first to either do or receive something. Concluding this section then, the gathering together of the chosen ones is the first event which Christ sends his angels to accomplish. The 144,000 and all of the alive people of Israel who have endured the tribulation and the reign of the Antichrist are gathered to Mount Zion to stand with the Lamb. They

---

[48] Bullinger, E.W. *A Critical Lexicon and Concordance*, p. 150.

are specially favored because of their faithful stand during the tribulation.

SATAN IS BOUND

Right after the end of the battles, the angel with the key to the bottomless pit lays hold on the Dragon, the Accuser, and he is bound for a thousand years.

Revelation 20:1-3 APNT
And I saw another angel that came down from heaven, who had
the key of the abyss and a great chain in his hand.
And he grabbed the dragon, the ancient serpent, who is the Accuser and Satan, and bound him [for] one thousand years.
And he threw him into the abyss and closed and sealed the top over
him, so that he would not seduce all the nations any more. After
these [things], he must release him [for] a short time.

The Devil is bound, cast into the bottomless pit, shut up, and a seal is set upon him. The abyss is literally "without bottom" and is also called "the deep." Its location is uncertain, but wherever it may be, the angel who binds him makes certain that the Devil will not deceive the nations anymore during those thousand years.

Jesus Christ proceeds to carry out the prophecies of judging the world, both the living and the dead.

Psalm 96:13 KJV
Before the Lord: For he cometh, for he cometh to judge the earth:
he shall judge the world with righteousness, and the people with
his truth.

JUDGMENT OF THE GENTILES

After Satan is chained and the battle finished, those Gentiles (of the nations) who are yet alive are judged according to how they treated Israel (the believers) during the whole tribulation time. This judgment takes place in the valley of Jehoshaphat.

Joel 3:1-2, 14 ESV
"For behold, in those days and at that time, when I restore the fortunes of Judah and Jerusalem,
I will gather all the nations and bring them down to the Valley of Jehoshaphat. And I will enter into judgment with them there, on behalf of my people and my heritage Israel, because they have scattered them among the nations and have divided up my land,
Multitudes, multitudes, in the valley of decision! For the day of the LORD is near in the valley of decision.

The valley of Jehoshaphat could be the opened valley by the city of Jerusalem or it could be the location where the battle against Edom was miraculously seen during Jehoshaphat's time, which is near En Gedi. Another viewpoint is that Jehoshaphat means, "Yahweh has judged," referring to a symbolical name. If all the rest of the nations who have not been killed in the war of the day of God Almighty come together somewhere, it will need to be a location large enough to accommodate all the people.

Matthew offers a detailed description of the judgment. Jesus Christ sits on a "throne of glory" and this judgment pertains to individual Gentiles.

Matthew 25:31-36 APNT
And when the Son of Man comes in his glory and all of his holy angels with him, then he will sit on the throne of his glory.

And all the nations will be gathered before him. And he will sepa-
rate them one from another as a shepherd who separates the sheep
from the goats.
And he will set the sheep on his right and the goats on his left.
Then the king will say to those who are on his right, 'Come,
blessed of my Father, inherit the kingdom that has been prepared
for you from the foundations of the world.'
For I was hungry and you gave me to eat. And I was thirsty and
you gave me to drink. I was a stranger and you took me in.
I was naked and you covered me. I was sick and you visited me.
And I was in prison and you came to me.

The Son of Man sits on a throne on the earth and does this judging personally. This is not a judgment for Israel, but a judgment of the rest of the Gentiles of the nations who are still alive. They are judged on how they treated Israel during the time of the tribulation. The punishment is the "everlasting fire" (Matthew 25:41) and the reward is "life eternal" (Matthew 25:46).

An image of "outer darkness" (Matthew 8:12) and "the blackness of darkness" is used with fire also.

2 Peter 2:17 APNT
These [men] are wells without water, clouds that are driven by a
whirlwind, those for whom the blackness of darkness is reserved.

The Dictionary of Biblical Imagery has a succinct explanation of the symbols of fire and darkness.

> The images of darkness and fire appear contradictory, but
> they should be regarded as symbols pointing to a reality
> more horrific than either symbol can convey by itself. In
> fact, biblical images of hell leave many details to the

imagination perhaps because no picture is capable of doing justice to the reality.[49]

The kingdom which the Gentile "sheep" inherit is the kingdom on earth, and they worship in Jerusalem during the thousand years.

RESURRECTION OF THE JUST

After the completion of the judgment of the Gentiles, the next thing which Christ does is to prepare the rest of Israel for the reign of the thousand years. This is when Israel from all of the prior time periods is raised. This resurrection is called the "resurrection of the just" (Luke 14:14, Acts 24:15), the "better resurrection" (Hebrews 11:35), "the resurrection of life" (John 5:29a), "the resurrection at the last day" (John 11:24), and the "first resurrection" (Revelation 20:6a). The term "first resurrection" can mean "earliest," but it can also describe having priority as "the first of place, order, time or dignity."[50] It is called "better" in Hebrews because participation in this resurrection indicates those who will receive the blessings of living and reigning with Christ for a thousand years. That is why the best title is resurrection of the just, for then there is no question which point in time is meant.

The resurrection of the just includes all those martyred during the tribulation. The vision of the great multitude of Revelation 7:9-17 fits here. These are given white robes and are mentioned specifically again in Revelation 20 to make certain that it is known they are in this resurrection.

---

[49] Ryken, Leland, ed. *Dictionary of Biblical Imagery*, p. 377.
[50] Bullinger, E.W. *A Critical Lexicon and Concordance to the English and Greek New Testament,* p.288.

Revelation 20:4-6 ESV
Then I saw thrones, and seated on them were those to whom the
authority to judge was committed. Also I saw the souls of those who
had been beheaded for the testimony of Jesus and for the word of
God, and those who had not worshiped the beast or its image and
had not received its mark on their foreheads or their hands. They
came to life and reigned with Christ for a thousand years.
The rest of the dead did not come to life until the thousand years
were ended. This is the first resurrection.
Blessed and holy is the one who shares in the first resurrection!
Over such the second death has no power, but they will be priests of
God and of Christ, and they will reign with him for a thousand years.

There are several other passages from the Old Testament that are
referring to this resurrection.

Isaiah 26:19 ESV
Your dead shall live; their bodies shall rise. You who dwell in the
dust, awake and sing for joy! For your dew is a dew of light, and
the earth will give birth to the dead.

Ezekiel 37 describes how the dead are made alive and what is their
reward. I want to include the whole passage here because it is such
a vivid description of how the dead will be raised to life.

Ezekiel 37:1-14 ESV
The hand of the LORD was upon me, and he brought me out in the
Spirit of the LORD and set me down in the middle of the valley; it
was full of bones.
And he led me around among them, and behold, there were very
many on the surface of the valley, and behold, they were very dry.
And he said to me, "Son of man, can these bones live?" And I an-
swered, "O Lord GOD, you know."

Then he said to me, "Prophesy over these bones, and say to them, O dry bones, hear the word of the LORD.

Thus says the Lord GOD to these bones: Behold, I will cause breath to enter you, and you shall live.

And I will lay sinews upon you, and will cause flesh to come upon you, and cover you with skin, and put breath in you, and you shall live, and you shall know that I am the LORD."

So I prophesied as I was commanded. And as I prophesied, there was a sound, and behold, a rattling, and the bones came together, bone to its bone.

And I looked, and behold, there were sinews on them, and flesh had come upon them, and skin had covered them. But there was no breath in them.

Then he said to me, "Prophesy to the breath; prophesy, son of man, and say to the breath, Thus says the Lord GOD: Come from the four winds, O breath, and breathe on these slain, that they may live."

So I prophesied as he commanded me, and the breath came into them, and they lived and stood on their feet, an exceedingly great army.

Then he said to me, "Son of man, these bones are the whole house of Israel. Behold, they say, 'Our bones are dried up, and our hope is lost; we are indeed cut off.'

Therefore prophesy, and say to them, Thus says the Lord GOD: Behold, I will open your graves and raise you from your graves, O my people. And I will bring you into the land of Israel.

And you shall know that I am the LORD, when I open your graves, and raise you from your graves, O my people.

And I will put my Spirit within you, and you shall live, and I will place you in your own land. Then you shall know that I am the LORD; I have spoken, and I will do it, declares the LORD."

God raises Israel from the grave, pours breath into them and then gives them the Spirit, as was prophesied in Joel.

THE KINGDOM ESTABLISHED

Joel 2:28-29 ESV
And it shall come to pass afterward, that I will pour out my Spirit on all flesh; your sons and your daughters shall prophesy, your old men shall dream dreams, and your young men shall see visions. Even on the male and female servants in those days I will pour out my Spirit.

Remember when we studied about the number of days that were described in Daniel? He alludes to the fact that there will be an additional 30 plus 45 days. The sanctuary is cleansed during this time (Daniel 8:13-14). And there are other cataclysmic changes to the earth to begin cleaning it up from the aftermath of the war and the tribulation. This is the time period of the establishing of the kingdom and includes the next event, which is the marriage supper of the Lamb.

> *Israel is the bride and the marriage supper is right before the kingdom begins. Israel will reign with Christ for a thousand years*

THE MARRIAGE SUPPER OF THE LAMB

During these extra 75 days, there is the celebration of the marriage feast. This topic has been widely disputed, not only about who the bride is, but also, when the marriage and the feast take place.

Revelation 19:9 APNT
And they said to me, "Write. Blessed [are] those who are invited [ones] to the supper of the marriage feast of the Lamb." And he said to me, "These are the true words of God."

The word *gamos* in Greek for "wedding supper" can be either the feast or the actual wedding. The Aramaic text makes it clearer that Revelation 19 is talking about the supper of the marriage feast, similar to what Jesus and his mother were celebrating in Cana in John 2.

The key to understanding who the bride is comes full circle back to the beginning chapter where we understood that the period of the Church of the Body was a mystery and this mystery did not end until the gathering together. Since the church now is called a "body" with Christ as the head, then we are part of the bridegroom, not the bride. Charles Capps explains this further:

> If the Church, the Body of Christ was identified as the Bride of Christ in Scripture, then we would not have the legal right to take on His identity or be considered ONE with Him. If we were only a bride, we would not even have the legal right to use His name until after the marriage actually took place.[51]

The bridegroom went to "prepare a place" for his bride when he ascended into heaven in Acts 1.

John 14:1-3 KJV
Let not your heart be troubled: ye believe in God, believe also in me.
In my Father's house are many mansions: if it were not so, I would have told you. I go to prepare a place for you.
And if I go and prepare a place for you, I will come again, and receive you unto myself; that where I am, there ye may be also.

---

[51] Capps, Charles. *End-Time Events*, pp. 123-124.

THE KINGDOM ESTABLISHED

The marriage customs of the first century consisted of the ceremony first and then a feast commenced for at least seven days. All of the friends of the bridegroom were invited to the supper. The actual consummation of the marriage did not happen until after this feast. That is the reason I have put this event in this particular place because the next event is the start of the Millennial Kingdom. The bride is escorted to the newly restored land of Israel and lives and reigns with the King for the next 1,000 years.

Although there is much written about brides in the Prophets, I have not included any of these verses because I am not sure how they fit with the description of the Lamb's wife. These verses are not explicit enough. This is the best information I know at the moment, but I will continue to look for further understanding in the future.

Nevertheless, there is so much we can know about the Millennial Kingdom right now! Are you ready for the climax of the movie?

CHAPTER 12 ⧧ THE MILLENNIAL REIGN OF CHRIST

Events	Scriptures
Changes in the Land	Daniel 2:44-45
	Micah 4:1-7
	Jeremiah 3:17
	Isaiah 35:5-10
	Isaiah 65:19-25
	Ezekiel 39:8-16
	Zechariah 14:16-19
	Psalm 2:8-9
Holy Oblation and the New Temple	Ezekiel 40-48
	Isaiah 56:7
	Isaiah 4:2-6

There are a number of terms used to describe the 1,000-year reign of Christ. One is Millennium, which is a term derived from the Latin *mille* meaning a thousand and *annum,* meaning years. Other synonyms for this time period are Millennial Kingdom, Messianic Kingdom, 1,000-year Reign of Christ and Messianic Age. I have chosen to call it the Millennial Reign of Christ because it emphasizes who the King is and that this is a Kingdom which will last for this 1,000-year period and beyond.

If you recall, in Daniel's vision of Nebuchadnezzar's statue, he described there would be a stone that would smash the statue and set up a kingdom that would never end.

Daniel 2:44-45 ESV
And in the days of those kings the God of heaven will set up a kingdom that shall never be destroyed, nor shall the kingdom be left to another people. It shall break in pieces all these kingdoms and bring them to an end, and it shall stand forever,

*just as you saw that a stone was cut from a mountain by no human
hand, and that it broke in pieces the iron, the bronze, the clay, the
silver, and the gold. A great God has made known to the king what
shall be after this. The dream is certain, and its interpretation
sure.*

Many have claimed that belief in a literal Millennial Reign of Christ
is a recent evangelical interpretation. But many of the earliest
Church fathers were pre-millennialists, including Papias, Justin, and
many more. That is, they expected the personal coming of Christ to
follow with a 1,000-year reign on the earth before the last judgment.
This was also the expectation of the Jewish rabbis and the teachers
according to their understanding of the prophecies from the Old Testament.

As previously explained in Chapter 2, the "times of the Gentiles"
has ended and the "time of the restitution of all things" has begun.

Acts 3:21 NASB
*whom heaven must receive until the period of restoration of all
things about which God spoke by the mouth of His holy prophets
from ancient time.*

Imagine a time when the world will be filled with righteousness,
goodness, total permanent peace and where there is no injustice! The
key reason this occurs is that the rule of Jesus Christ, both spiritually
and literally, is over the entire earth. He reigns on the throne of
David and fulfills the promise to David that his seed would reign
forever. The capital of the kingdom will be Jerusalem. The city will
be set on the highest mountain and greatly expanded. Many passages
describe these changes, but one of my favorites is from Micah.

THE MILLENNIAL REIGN OF CHRIST

Micah 4:1-7 NET
In the future the LORD's Temple Mount will be the most important
mountain of all; it will be more prominent than other hills. People
will stream to it.
Many nations will come, saying, "Come on! Let's go up to the
LORD's mountain, to the temple of Jacob's God, so he can teach
us his commands and we can live by his laws." For Zion will be
the source of instruction; the LORD's teachings will proceed from
Jerusalem.
He will arbitrate between many peoples and settle disputes be-
tween many distant nations. They will beat their swords into plow-
shares, and their spears into pruning hooks. Nations will not use
weapons against other nations, and they will no longer train for
war.
Each will sit under his own grapevine or under his own fig tree
without any fear. The LORD who commands armies has decreed it.
Though all the nations follow their respective gods, we will follow
the LORD our God forever.
"In that day," says the LORD, "I will gather the lame, and assem-
ble the outcasts whom I injured.
I will transform the lame into the nucleus of a new nation, and
those far off into a mighty nation. The LORD will reign over them
on Mount Zion, from that day forward and forevermore."

Jesus Christ will rule over the nations from Jerusalem and all the
nations will come and honor him.

Jeremiah 3:17 NLT
In that day Jerusalem will be known as 'The Throne of the LORD.'
All nations will come there to honor the LORD. They will no
longer stubbornly follow their own evil desires.

THE MILLENNIAL REIGN OF CHRIST

The heavens and the earth are restored to idyllic conditions. The seasons, sun and moon are changed and cause the land to prosper. There will still be work, but it will be fulfilling and easy.

Isaiah 30:26 KJV
Moreover the light of the moon shall be as the light of the sun, and the light of the sun shall be sevenfold, as the light of seven days, in the day that the Lord bindeth up the breach of his people, and healeth the stroke of their wound.

The waters are healed and there is a great abundance of food. Trees bear fruit every month instead of only once a year. The waters of the Dead Sea will be healed and many fish will be found in it again. Good news for those who love to fish!

Ezekiel 47:6-12 NET
He said to me, "Son of man, have you seen this?" Then he led me back to the bank of the river.
When I had returned, I noticed a vast number of trees on the banks of the river, on both sides.
He said to me, "These waters go out toward the eastern region and flow down into the Arabah; when they enter the Dead Sea, where the sea is stagnant, the waters become fresh.
Every living creature which swarms where the river flows will live; there will be many fish, for these waters flow there. It will become fresh and everything will live where the river flows.
Fishermen will stand beside it; from Engedi to En-eglaim they will spread nets. They will catch many kinds of fish, like the fish of the Great Sea.
But its swamps and its marshes will not become fresh; they will re-main salty.
On both sides of the river's banks, every kind of tree will grow for food. Their leaves will not wither nor will their fruit fail, but they will bear fruit every month, because their water source flows from

145

the sanctuary. Their fruit will be for food and their leaves for healing."

Revelation describes the river that pours out from the throne of God and the Lamb.

Revelation 22:1-4 NET
Then the angel showed me the river of the water of life– water as clear as crystal– pouring out from the throne of God and of the Lamb,
flowing down the middle of the city's main street. On each side of the river is the tree of life producing twelve kinds of fruit, yielding its fruit every month of the year. Its leaves are for the healing of the nations.
And there will no longer be any curse, and the throne of God and the Lamb will be in the city. His servants will worship him,
and they will see his face, and his name will be on their foreheads.

Many aspects of the curse Adam received will be reversed. People will be healed. The desert will bloom and the animals will not kill each other.

Isaiah 35:5-10 NET
Then blind eyes will open, deaf ears will hear.
Then the lame will leap like a deer, the mute tongue will shout for joy; for water will flow in the desert, streams in the wilderness.
The dry soil will become a pool of water, the parched ground springs of water. Where jackals once lived and sprawled out, grass, reeds, and papyrus will grow.
A thoroughfare will be there– it will be called the Way of Holiness. The unclean will not travel on it; it is reserved for those authorized to use it– fools will not stray into it.

No lions will be there, no ferocious wild animals will be on it— they will not be found there. Those delivered from bondage will travel on it,
those whom the LORD has ransomed will return that way. They will enter Zion with a happy shout. Unending joy will crown them, happiness and joy will overwhelm them; grief and suffering will disappear.

People will live to be a hundred years or more. The lion will lay down with the lamb. Amazing!! There are many characteristics of this time. One of the most outstanding is that there will be no more weeping and sorrow.

Isaiah 65:19-25 NET
"Jerusalem will bring me joy, and my people will bring me happiness. The sound of weeping or cries of sorrow will never be heard in her again.
Never again will one of her infants live just a few days or an old man die before his time. Indeed, no one will die before the age of a hundred, anyone who fails to reach the age of a hundred will be considered cursed.
They will build houses and live in them; they will plant vineyards and eat their fruit.
No longer will they build a house only to have another live in it, or plant a vineyard only to have another eat its fruit, for my people will live as long as trees, and my chosen ones will enjoy to the fullest what they have produced.
They will not work in vain, or give birth to children that will experience disaster. For the LORD will bless their children and their descendants.
Before they even call out, I will respond; while they are still speaking, I will hear.

*A wolf and a lamb will graze together; a lion, like an ox, will eat
straw, and a snake's food will be dirt. They will no longer injure or
destroy on my entire royal mountain," says the LORD.*

There is a period of time which is necessary to accomplish these
changes. Because of the carnage from the battle in the area southeast
of the Dead Sea, there will be some cleanup that occurs as described
in Ezekiel 39. First of all, the weapons will be burned and the remnant used for firewood for the next seven years.

Ezekiel 39:8-10 NASB
*"Behold, it is coming and it shall be done," declares the Lord
God. "That is the day of which I have spoken.*
*"Then those who inhabit the cities of Israel will go out, and make
fires with the weapons and burn them, both shields and bucklers,
bows and arrows, war clubs and spears and for seven years they
will make fires of them.*
*"And they will not take wood from the field or gather firewood
from the forests, for they will make fires with the weapons; and
they will take the spoil of those who despoiled them, and seize the
plunder of those who plundered them," declares the Lord God.*

For the first seven months, the people of Israel are busy burying the
bones left from the battle of Gog and Mag. After the end of seven
months, they continue to search for bones left in the land. If anyone
finds a bone, they must set up a sign by it until those doing the
burying come and bury it.

Ezekiel 39:11-16 KJV
*And it shall come to pass in that day, that I will give unto Gog a
place there of graves in Israel, the valley of the passengers on the
east of the sea: and it shall stop the noses of the passengers: and
there shall they bury Gog and all his multitude: and they shall call
it The valley of Hamongog.*

And seven months shall the house of Israel be burying of them, that they may cleanse the land.

Yea, all the people of the land shall bury them; and it shall be to them a renown the day that I shall be glorified, saith the Lord GOD.

And they shall sever out men of continual employment, passing through the land to bury with the passengers those that remain upon the face of the earth, to cleanse it: after the end of seven months shall they search.

And the passengers that pass through the land, when any seeth a man's bone, then shall he set up a sign by it, till the buriers have buried it in the valley of Hamongog.

And also the name of the city shall be Hamonah. Thus shall they cleanse the land.

The name Hamongog means "the multitude of Gog" and the city is called Hamonah, a feminine form of the word meaning horde or multitude. In Ezekiel 39:11-15 "there is a play on words—there were 'passengers' to be buried, 'passengers' to walk over their graves, 'passengers' to bury them; (or, a play upon the treble meaning of passing in (invading), passing by, and passing through.)"[52] It will be near the "valley of the passengers" which is an allusion to a valley through which travelers used to pass on their way from Syria, Babylon and other northern locations to Egypt and Arabia. Today there is a main highway that follows north and south along the ancient road.

THE KINGDOM POPULATION

Three categories of people populate the Kingdom: 1) Christians of the gathering together with their new spiritual bodies, 2) Israel who are raised during the resurrection of the just, and 3) "natural" or mortal people who were judged righteous in the judgment of the

---

[52] Barnes, Albert, *Notes on the Bible*, Ezekiel 39.

Gentiles. This last category are the people who will make up the nations. Because there is no war and plenty of food, these survivors will multiply rapidly and repopulate the earth.

The nations which are left outside the land of Israel are required to come up and worship at Jerusalem. If they do not come for the Feast of Tabernacles, no rain will fall on their lands.

Zechariah 14:16-19 ESV
Then everyone who survives of all the nations that have come against Jerusalem shall go up year after year to worship the King, the LORD of hosts, and to keep the Feast of Booths.
And if any of the families of the earth do not go up to Jerusalem to worship the King, the LORD of hosts, there will be no rain on them.
And if the family of Egypt does not go up and present themselves, then on them there shall be no rain; there shall be the plague with which the LORD afflicts the nations that do not go up to keep the Feast of Booths.
This shall be the punishment to Egypt and the punishment to all the nations that do not go up to keep the Feast of Booths.

This is the fulfillment also of Psalm 2, where the heathen (Gentile nations) are given to Christ for an inheritance.

Psalms 2:8-9 KJV
Ask of me, and I shall give thee the heathen for thine inheritance, and the uttermost parts of the earth for thy possession.
Thou shalt break them with a rod of iron; thou shalt dash them in pieces like a potter's vessel.

Christ will rule the nations with a rod of iron. The need for the rod of iron is due to the natural people who still have a sin nature causing them to be selfish and sinful even without the temptations of the Evil One.

This is just a brief view of things which will occur at this time. There is a wonderful chapter in the book, *Things To Come*, by J. Dwight Pentecost, where he documents conditions of the Millennium with corresponding scriptures.[53]

THE HOLY OBLATION AND THE NEW TEMPLE

The land and the city of Jerusalem are prepared for the reign of Christ. A new temple is built which is described in detail in Ezekiel. The land is apportioned to the 12 tribes and special areas are allocated for the Prince, and to the Levites and priests.

When Joshua divided the Promised Land among the tribes of Israel, the amount of land for each tribe was uneven in size and shape. In the Millennial Kingdom, the land will be divided into equal strips going widthwise from east to west. The Kingdom will be the fulfillment of the promise to Abraham of the land. There are a number of interpretations of the exact extent of the promise of the land.

Genesis 15:18 ESV
On that day the LORD made a covenant with Abram, saying, "To your offspring I give this land, from the river of Egypt to the great river, the river Euphrates."

Most scholars show only the west side of the Sea of Galilee and the Dead Sea (or sometimes include just a small area east of the Jordan River) as the portion of the land. Clarence Larkin has an illustration showing that the land goes as far north as the Euphrates River and as far south as Egypt. The east side border is not defined in this

---

[53] Pentecost, J. Dwight. *Things to Come*, pp. 476-490.

picture which I believe represents a clearer view of the extent of the land allotted to Israel.

Moses received a description of the land allotted to Israel in broad terms.

Exodus 23:31 ESV
And I will set your border from the Red Sea to the Sea of the Philistines, and from the wilderness to the Euphrates, for I will give the inhabitants of the land into your hand, and you shall drive them out before you.

I believe the land given to Abraham does go eastward past the Dead Sea and perhaps all the way to the Euphrates River. How that will be unfolded in the Millennial Reign of Christ remains to be seen.

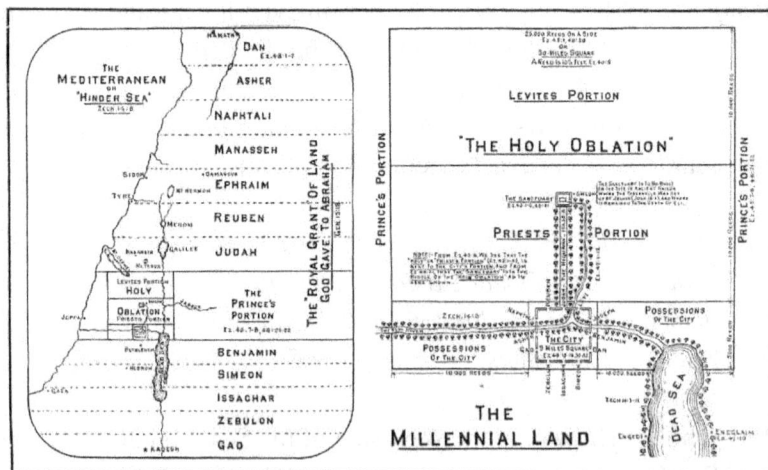

The picture to the right of the land is an expanded picture of what is called the "Holy Oblation." It consists of four sections: the Levites' portion, the Priests' portion with the temple in the center, the city of

Jerusalem itself with its outlying areas and the Prince's portion. The river runs from the south side of the temple and flows west to the Mediterranean Sea and east to the Dead Sea.[54]

In a series of visions to Ezekiel, the measurements of the city, the portions and the temple are meticulously laid out. The measuring unit used called a "reed" consists of six Hebrew "long" cubits, a cubit (about 18 inches) and a handbreadth (about 3 inches), for a total of 21 inches. Therefore, the measuring reed in the man's hand was 10.5 feet (3.15 meters) long.

Ezekiel 40:5 ESV
And behold, there was a wall all around the outside of the temple area, and the length of the measuring reed in the man's hand was six long cubits, each being a cubit and a handbreadth in length. So he measured the thickness of the wall, one reed; and the height, one reed.

The King James Version calls this area an "oblation." This is the Hebrew word, *teruwmah,* and is used of the heave offering and any portion that is set aside as "holy" to God. These heave offerings were for the use of the priesthood. Here it does not mean an offering, but a grant of land.

Ezekiel 45:1 KJV
Moreover, when ye shall divide by lot the land for inheritance, ye shall offer an oblation unto the LORD, an holy portion of the land: the length shall be the length of five and twenty thousand reeds, and the breadth shall be ten thousand. This shall be holy in all the borders thereof round about.

---

[54] Larkin, Clarence, *The Book of Revelation*, p. 185.

In the KJV, the word for "reeds" is in italics, meaning that it is added to the translation. And on further investigation, other descriptions in Ezekiel 48 also do not have a Hebrew word defining what the 25,000 measurement is referring to. Most of the older translations choose *reeds*, and the newer translations choose *cubits*. If cubits is used, the width is approximately 8¼ miles by 6 2/3 miles. The Septuagint offers no clarification of the measurement. Using cubits as the measurement results in a relatively small area to enclose all of the city, the sanctuary and the Priests' and Levites' portions. But if reeds is selected, then the extent of the holy portion is 50 miles by 50 miles.

The New Treasury of Scripture Knowledge explains the logic as follows:

> These three formed the square of 25,000 reeds, or nearly fifty miles; and that set apart for the price, the breadth of which is not mentioned, extended in length from north to south, along the east and west sides of the square. As Canaan would not admit of so large a portion for the sanctuary, etc., this was no doubt intended to intimate the large extent of the church in the glorious times predicted. …it is possible to take these predictions literally since Israel will then possess all of the land originally promised to Abraham, and certain geographical changes will doubtless make a literal fulfillment of the prophecy entirely possible.[55]

The following is a chart of this holy portion of the land using the measurement of a reed being 10.5 feet.

---

[55] Smith, Jerome H. *The New Treasury of Scripture Knowledge*, p. 938.

LEVITES' PORTION

25,000 REEDS X 10,000 REEDS
50 MILES X 20 MILES

PRINCE'S PORTION

PRINCE'S PORTION

PRIESTS' PORTION

25,000 REEDS X 10,000 REEDS
50 MILES X 20 MILES

TEMPLE

| CITY DISTRICT FOR CROPS ON EACH SIDE OF CITY 20 MILES X 10 MILES | CITY OF JERUSALEM 10 MILES SQUARE | CITY DISTRICT FOR CROPS ON EACH SIDE OF CITY 20 MILES X 10 MILES |

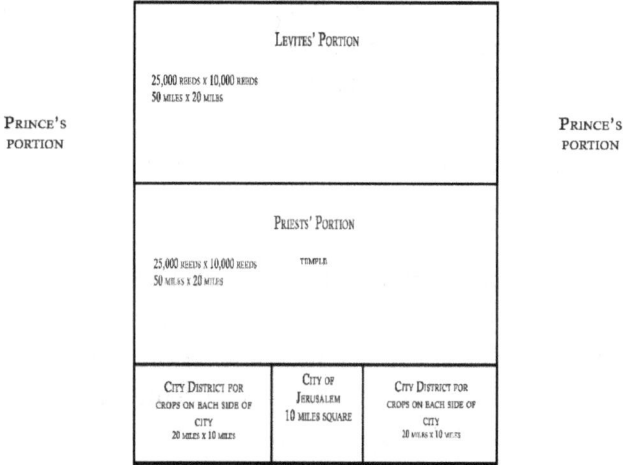

Ezekiel 48:35 KJV
It was round about eighteen thousand measures: and the name of the city from that day shall be, The LORD is there.

Jerusalem will be called "Jehovah Shammah," the Lord is present.

The temple is in the middle of the Priests' Portion. Some interpret Ezekiel by putting the Priests' portion as the northernmost section. This would position the temple about 30 miles from the outskirts of Jerusalem. I have chosen to side with older commentaries on this.

The Prince's Portion is on both sides of the "holy portion" east and west to both seas. Who is this "Prince" exactly? This is also a matter of some debate. It has been thought that it refers to Christ, but why he would need a special area of land is not explained. The best interpretation I have read is that he is of the house of David as a ruler over the people.

> The prince must mean the civil ruler under Messiah. His connection with the east gate (by which the Lord had

returned to His temple) implies, that, as ruling under God, he is to stand in a place of peculiar nearness to God. He represents Messiah, who entered heaven, the true sanctuary, by a way that none other could, namely, by His own holiness; all others must enter as sinners by faith in His blood, through grace.[56]

There are a number of key differences between this temple and the previous ones of Solomon and Herod. Absent are the ark of the covenant, the menorah, the showbread, the altar of incense and the laver. Jesus Christ is not only the King but also the High Priest. Since he has fulfilled all the foreshadowing of these from the Old Testament, there is no more need for them. There is no veil, no court of the Gentiles or court of the women. All are welcome to come into the sanctuary area.

Zechariah 6:12-13 ESV
And say to him, "Thus says the LORD of hosts, "Behold, the man whose name is the Branch: for he shall branch out from his place, and he shall build the temple of the LORD.
It is he who shall build the temple of the LORD and shall bear royal honor, and shall sit and rule on his throne. And there shall be a priest on his throne, and the counsel of peace shall be between them both."

There is only one large altar called the "table of the LORD" located in the Holy Place.

Ezekiel 41:22 NET
The altar was of wood, 5¼ feet high, with its length 3½ feet; its corners, its length, and its walls were of wood. He said to me, "This is the table that is before the LORD."

---

[56] James, Fausset, Brown *Commentary on the Whole Bible*, p. 727.

The Priests minister at the altar and there are sacrifices and offerings similar to those of the Mosaic Law. However, these sacrifices are looking backward as memorials to Jesus Christ's perfect fulfillment of all of the Law. The temple is called "a house of prayer."

Isaiah 56:7 ESV
these I will bring to my holy mountain, and make them joyful in my house of prayer; their burnt offerings and their sacrifices will be accepted on my altar; for my house shall be called a house of prayer for all peoples.

E.W. Bullinger in Appendix **88** of *The Companion Bible* has a beautiful illustration of Ezekiel's temple.

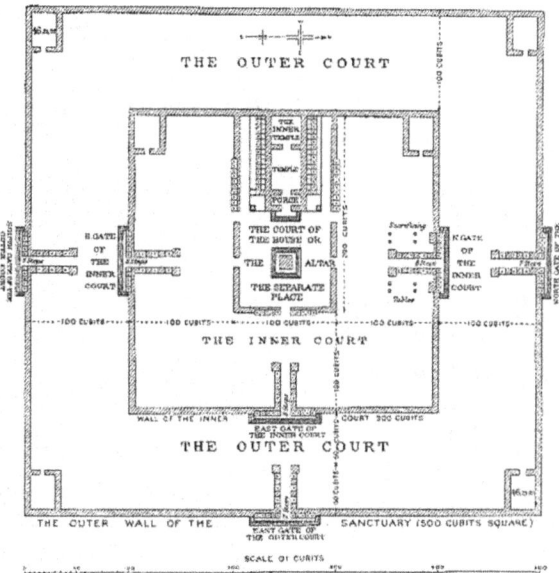

The temple was 500 cubits square with open space surrounding it. The temple was approximately one mile on each side. John W. Schmitt provides a wonderful reference with many illustrations of the interior of the temple in his book called *Messiah's Coming Temple.*

The temple is filled with the Shekinah Glory of the Lord as in the early days of Solomon.

Ezekiel 43:4-9 NASB
And the glory of the LORD came into the house by the way of the gate facing toward the east.
And the Spirit lifted me up and brought me into the inner court; and behold, the glory of the LORD filled the house.
Then I heard one speaking to me from the house, while a man was standing beside me.
And He said to me, "Son of man, this is the place of My throne and the place of the soles of My feet, where I will dwell among the sons of Israel forever. And the house of Israel will not again defile My holy name, neither they nor their kings, by their harlotry and by the corpses of their kings when they die,
by setting their threshold by My threshold, and their door post beside My door post, with only the wall between Me and them. And they have defiled My holy name by their abominations which they have committed. So I have consumed them in My anger.
Now let them put away their harlotry and the corpses of their kings far from Me; and I will dwell among them forever."

There will a be a cloud by day and pillar of fire by night over the whole site of Mount Zion similar to what God provided for the children of Israel in the wilderness.

Isaiah 4:2-6 NASB
In that day the Branch of the LORD will be beautiful and glorious, and the fruit of the earth will be the pride and the adornment of the survivors of Israel.

And it will come about that he who is left in Zion and remains in Jerusalem will be called holy– everyone who is recorded for life in Jerusalem.

When the Lord has washed away the filth of the daughters of Zion, and purged the bloodshed of Jerusalem from her midst, by the spirit of judgment and the spirit of burning,

then the LORD will create over the whole area of Mount Zion and over her assemblies a cloud by day, even smoke, and the brightness of a flaming fire by night; for over all the glory will be a canopy.

And there will be a shelter to give shade from the heat by day, and refuge and protection from the storm and the rain.

Isn't that beautiful? The temple, the newly rebuilt city of Jerusalem and its surrounding areas will be a source of great joy and a place of celebration for all of the feasts. People will stream into Mount Zion to be blessed by the presence of the Lord.

CHAPTER 13 ⚏ THE TELOS

Events	Scriptures
Satan loosed and deceives the nations	Revelation 20:7-8
Fire from God consumes the enemies	Revelation 20:9
Devil cast into the lake of fire and brimstone to be tormented forever	Revelation 20:10 Ezekiel 28:17-19
Resurrection of the unjust Great white throne judgment	Revelation 20:11-13 2 Peter 2:9
Death and the grave and all judged as wicked cast in lake of fire	Revelation 20:14-15 1 Corinthians 15:24-28
Heavens and earth dissolved, the end of the day of the Lord	2 Peter 3:10-12
New heavens and earth	2 Peter 3:13 Revelation 21:1-5 Isaiah 65:17

After the thousand years are finished, Satan is loosed for a little season. He goes out to deceive the nations and gathers them to battle AGAIN! The same nations of Gog and Magog as in the battle right before the Millennium are at the forefront.

Revelation 20:7-8 APNT
And when one thousand years is completed, Satan will be released from his imprisonment
and will go out to seduce all the nations in the four corners of the earth, to Gog and to Magog, and to assemble them for battle, whose number [is] as the sand of the sea.

However, before they accomplish anything, God sends fire from heaven and they are devoured. The word for "consumed" in both Greek and Aramaic means to consume by eating up completely. They do not even have a chance to do any more evil!

Revelation 20:9 APNT
And they went up on the space of the land and surrounded the city
of the camp of the holy [ones] and the beloved city and fire came
down from heaven from God and consumed them.

The only things left to be accomplished are the final demise of the
Devil and his angels and the second resurrection. After the Devil's
final deceptive attempt fails, the time for his destruction is at hand.

Revelation 20:10 APNT
And the Accuser, their seducer, was thrown into the lake of fire
and sulfur, where the creature and the false prophet [were]. And
they will be tormented, day and night, forever and ever.

This torment is not unending, but as we saw in Chapter 2, "forever
and ever" means *to the limit of our sight and beyond.* Actually, the
Devil is destroyed by the utter evil of his own nature within him. He
will exist no more and will certainly not be part of the new heavens
and earth.

Ezekiel 28:17-19 KJV
Thine heart was lifted up because of thy beauty, thou hast cor-
rupted thy wisdom by reason of thy brightness: I will cast thee to
the ground, I will lay thee before kings, that they may behold thee.
Thou hast defiled thy sanctuaries by the multitude of thine iniqui-
ties, by the iniquity of thy traffick; therefore will I bring forth a fire
from the midst of thee, it shall devour thee, and I will bring thee to
ashes upon the earth in the sight of all them that behold thee.
All they that know thee among the people shall be astonished at
thee: thou shalt be a terror, and never shalt thou be any more.

All believers from the Church of the Body and the first resurrection
are alive and present at this event and they will have the joyful
privilege of seeing the Evil One destroyed.

At this point, the beast, the false prophet, the Gentile nations from the judgment of the nations, and the Devil are all cast into the lake of fire. Others will join them after the resurrection of the unjust.

RESURRECTION OF THE UNJUST

After the Devil is cast into the lake of fire, then the rest of the dead are raised and judged out of the "books." They are judged according to their works.

Revelation 20:11-13 APNT
And I saw a large white throne and him who sat on top of it, from before whose face the earth and heaven fled away, and a place was not found for them.
And I saw the dead, great and small, who stood before the throne, and the scrolls were opened. And another scroll was opened that is [the one] of judgment, and the dead were judged from those [things] that were written in the scroll, according to their works.
And the sea gave up the dead in it and death and Sheol gave up the dead with them and each one of them was judged according to their works.

This scroll is not the same as the "Lamb's book of life" mentioned in Revelation 13:8. The Greek text says the "books" (plural) were opened, and another book was opened which is the book of life. "Book" is an *ellipsis*, meaning there is no word for book in the text. The Greek text also states that men are judged out of the "books" (plural). However, the Aramaic Peshitta makes it clear that this new scroll that is opened is one of judgment, not of "life" and it is this book (singular) that is used to judge people according to their works.

Revelation 20:12 KJV
And I saw the dead, small and great, stand before God; and the books were opened: and another book was opened, which is the

book of life: and the dead were judged out of those things which
were written in the books, according to their works.

The Codex Sinaiticus, which is one of the oldest Greek manuscripts found to date, further clarifies verse 13 as: "they were condemned, every one, according to their deeds."[57] This resurrection is called the second death in verse 14. The dead are raised only to be judged and then die again in the lake of fire. A literal translation of verse 14 reads as follows: "this is the second death, the lake of fire."[58]

Revelation 20:14-15 APNT
And death and Sheol were thrown into the lake of fire. This is the
second death.
And he who was not found inscribed in the book of life was thrown
into the lake of fire.

Here the book of life is mentioned as another criterion for judgment of whether a person is to be thrown into the lake of fire or not. It is possible that not all people in this resurrection will be condemned. If they ARE in the book of life, they will be spared. This time period is called the day of judgment in 2 Peter.

2 Peter 2:9 NET
if so, then the Lord knows how to rescue the godly from their tri-
als, and to reserve the unrighteous for punishment at the day of
judgment,

God is the supreme judge in all the judgments. He is featured particularly here on his great white throne because this is the final victory and final step to his plan of redemption for mankind.

---

[57] Seiss, Joseph, *The Apocalypse*, p. 480.
[58] Bullinger, E.W. *Commentary on Revelation*, p. 643.

THE TELOS

The last enemy, death, is now destroyed and all enemies are subject to Christ. This is the end, the *telos*, the very final end point of the ages.

1 Corinthians 15:24-28 APNT
And then will be the end, when he delivers the kingdom to God the Father, when every ruler and every authority and all powers cease.
For he is going to reign, until he places all his enemies under his feet.
And the last enemy, death, will be abolished.
FOR HE HAS SUBJECTED ALL UNDER HIS FEET. But when he says that everything has been made subject to him, it is evident that it is apart from him who subjected all to him.
And when everything is subjected to him, then the Son will be made subject to the one who subjected all to him, so that God will be all in all.

This is the final period of the day of the Lord that began with the great signs. This is also the very end point of the day of the Lord when the present heavens and earth are dissolved. This *telos* point is also called the "day of God" because during it, God is supreme.

2 Peter 3:10-12 APNT
But the day of the LORD will come as a thief, in which the heaven[s] will suddenly pass away and the elements, while burning, will dissolve and the earth and the works that are in it will [not] be found.
Since therefore all these [things] will be dissolved, how ought you to be in your conduct? [You should be] holy [ones] and with reverence for God,

while you expect and you desire the coming of the day of God, in which the heaven[s], being tried by fire, will be dissolved and the elements, while burning, will melt.

> ⚷
>
> *The telos is the end point of the day of the Lord and is also called the day of God*

After this, a perfected state is introduced. It is the new heavens and earth and paradise on earth once again.

2 Peter 3:13 ESV
But according to his promise we are waiting for new heavens and a new earth in which righteousness dwells.

There will be no more death or sorrow or pain.

Revelation 21:1-5 APNT
And I saw a new heaven and a new earth, for the former heaven and the former earth had gone away and there was no more sea. And I saw the holy city, the new Jerusalem, come down from heaven from God, prepared as a bride adorned for her husband. And I heard a loud voice from heaven that said, "Behold, the dwelling of God [is] with men, and he [will] live with them and they will be his own people and God is with them and will be a God to them.
And he will wipe all tears from their eyes and there will no longer be death, neither sorrow, nor crying, nor will there be any more pain on account of him,"
and it went away. And he who sat on the throne said to me, "Behold, I am making all [things] new." And he said to me, "Write. These words are faithful and true."

The Bible does not offer much information regarding the new heavens and earth. But we do know from the Scriptures that the former things will not be remembered. Such a day to look forward to!

Isaiah 65:17 KJV
For, behold, I create new heavens and a new earth: and the former shall not be remembered, nor come into mind.

Many more things could be expounded on from both the Prophets and Revelation. But even after this a brief explanation of the events of the end times, one can concur with the apostle John in Revelation 22:20, "Even so, come Lord Jesus!"

CHAPTER 14 ✦ THE HOPE OF HIS CALLING

Hope in God gives a person strength and unshakeable confidence. What God has promised, he will surely bring to pass. As we have explored the sequence of the events of the end times, perhaps you may have asked, "Why do I even need to know this?" This may have occurred especially in the section on the wrath of God! But that section is the one that we need to understand the most. Why? Because it reveals that even during the darkest of days, God still holds the promised future. He only allows the darkness to be prolonged so that every man, woman and child has an opportunity to repent. This is called God's longsuffering.

2 Peter 3:9 APNT
The LORD does not delay in his promises as men consider delay, but he is long-suffering because of you, in that he does not want anyone to be destroyed, but rather [that] everyone should come to repentance.

Longsuffering is not a term we normally use in our everyday vocabulary. But in American slang, phrases such as, "hang in there," "don't give up," and "keep on holding on" are indicative of the meaning of the term. The word longsuffering in Aramaic is actually an idiom (such as we have in English) and literally means, "long (or length) of spirit." The emphasis is on the word "long." The Hebrew phrase for longsuffering is also an idiom and is literally, "long of nose (or breathing)" and "as anger was indicated by rapid, violent breathing through the nostrils, 'long of anger,' or 'slow to wrath.'"[59] Thus the idea of longsuffering is that wrath is long in coming and is held back until there is no further choice.

---

[59] *International Standard Bible Dictionary*, longsuffering.

This was true in the days of Noah also. God waited 120 years and preached "righteousness" to the people, waiting for any others to repent. No one else repented, so only eight people were saved from the flood.

1 Peter 3:20 APNT
those who previously were disobedient in the days of Noah, when
[in] the long-suffering of God he commanded an ark to be made,
in hope of their repentance, yet only eight souls entered it and
were kept alive on the water.

We read previously in Luke that as it was in the days of Noah, so it will be in the end times. People will be eating and drinking and living their lives with no thought about what will happen in the future. Then the day of the Lord will come as a thief in the night and surprise everyone. But actually, for those who know what the Bible says about the end times, there will not be any doubt that all God said about the "last days" is going to come to pass.

God desires everyone to be saved and to come to him. He does not delay (or is not "slack" in his promises), as others regard delay. I have heard many people say during past years, "Why is God holding back? Why doesn't he just send his Son back and get this all over with?" He does not do things in our timeframe, but in HIS. And he knows exactly the right moment when the "times of the Gentiles" will be over, when the "times of restitution" will begin and when the new heavens and earth will be established.

REJOICE IN HOPE

We have hope so that we can rejoice. And we rejoice that we will see the glory of God!

THE HOPE OF HIS CALLING

Romans 5:2 ESV
*Through him we have also obtained access by faith into this grace
in which we stand, and we rejoice in hope of the glory of God.*

The word for hope in Aramaic is *savra* and it means to "look expectantly." Hope is something that a person needs to hold fast in
their mind and constantly review. We can actually hold fast to boasting about what will happen in the future because of this hope.

Hebrews 3:6 APNT
*Now Christ, as the Son, [is] over his house. And we are his house,
if we hold fast the boldness and the boasting of his hope to the end.*

God will reveal who his children really are in the future. We have
so much to look forward to—that is why we can rejoice! Even the
creation is eagerly waiting for "that day."

Romans 8:19-25 NLT
*For all creation is waiting eagerly for that future day when God
will reveal who his children really are.*
*Against its will, all creation was subjected to God's curse. But
with eager hope,*
*the creation looks forward to the day when it will join God's chil-
dren in glorious freedom from death and decay.*
*For we know that all creation has been groaning as in the pains of
childbirth right up to the present time.*
*And we believers also groan, even though we have the Holy Spirit
within us as a foretaste of future glory, for we long for our bodies
to be released from sin and suffering. We, too, wait with eager
hope for the day when God will give us our full rights as his
adopted children, including the new bodies he has promised us.
We were given this hope when we were saved. (If we already have
something, we don't need to hope for it.*

But if we look forward to something we don't yet have, we must wait patiently and confidently.)

We must wait with patience and confidence for the hope of the Gospel to come to pass.

Colossians 1:23 APNT
Since [this is so], continue in your faith, your foundation being firm, and be not shaken from the hope of the gospel that you heard [and] that was preached in all the creation that is under heaven, of which I, Paul, am a minister.

"Be not shaken" is the same verb used in Hebrews 6 where hope is called an "anchor" for our soul. Another noun from this verb is the word for "earthquake."

Hebrew 6:18-19 APNT
that by two things that are unchangeable in which God is not able to lie, we who have sought refuge in him may have great comfort and may hold fast to the hope that was promised to us, which we have as an anchor that holds our soul, so that it is not shaken and it enters within the veil,

The phrase "it enters within the veil" refers to the curtain in the temple that separated the Holy of Holies from the rest of the people. But what does it mean in this verse? The New Living Translation makes it much clearer.

Hebrews 6:19-20 NLT
This hope is a strong and trustworthy anchor for our souls. It leads us through the curtain into God's inner sanctuary.
Jesus has already gone in there for us. He has become our eternal High Priest in the order of Melchizedek.

Hope becomes an anchor to the soul in God's inner sanctuary. Jesus Christ opened the pathway to the presence of God which is represented by the Holy of Holies. It is now available for us to rest in that place. We have great confidence because of our relationship with the God who promised all of what will happen in the future. That is also why we do not need to fear the future, even in our lifetime now. We live patiently today, while waiting for the promises of God to come to pass.

Hope becomes an anchor to the soul in God's inner sanctuary

THE PROMISE OF GOD

There is a distinction in the words for promise in the Aramaic that sheds light on the meaning of how we share in the promise of Abraham. Abraham was the father of faith and we are the heirs of the promise made to him. What is this promise?

In Greek there is only one word for "to promise" or "promise." In Aramaic there are two words, and they are not used interchangeably. This is noteworthy because when comparing the two languages, the majority of the time there is more than one Greek word used for a single Aramaic word. When the opposite is true, it is important to find out why.

The two words for "promise" in Aramaic are *shudaya* and *mulkana*. We will look at *shudaya* first. *Shudaya* is formed from the Shaphel (intensive) tense of the verb *yada*. *Yada* means to profess, confess or promise. *Shudaya*, which is the noun, means a promise, declaration (a confession intensified) which has a manifested result or fulfillment. The emphasis and distinction of this word for promise is on the result or fulfillment.

1 Timothy 4:8 APNT
For the training of the body profits a little [time], but uprightness profits in everything and has the promise [shudaya] of the life of this time and of the future.

Godliness is profitable for all things. In other words, it shows results or an outward fulfillment in life now and also in the one to come. The emphasis is on the fulfillment, and not necessarily on the declaration of the promise.

Shudaya is used of "the promise of the Father" (Acts 1:4) and the promise of the Holy Spirit (Acts 2:33, 39 and Galatians 3:14). The promise of Holy Spirit was fulfilled on the day of Pentecost and the manifested result was speaking in tongues and magnifying God. This was the outward witness that God's promise had come true.

Mulkana, on the other hand, is from the verb *melak*. This verb means to counsel or advise in only four verses. In the rest of the verses where it appears it means to promise, to make an arbitrary declaration from an absolute owner. An example is a decree issued from a king or president. In fact, other nouns that are derived from this verb are king, queen, kingdom and decree. In this sense, the promise is unearned and not dependent on anything other than the one who declares it. Here are two verses that use this verb for promise.

Titus 1:2 APNT
concerning the hope of eternal life, which the true God promised [melak] before the times of the age.

Hebrews 10:23 APNT
And we should persist in the confession of our hope and we should
not waver, for he is faithful who promised [melak] us.

The one who is promising has the absolute authority to do so and it
is his job to ensure that the declaration comes to pass. The emphasis
then is on the declaration and not the fulfillment.

The noun *mulkana* is this kind of promise that is an absolute declaration. It also has an added definition of the promise having to do
with lands, property or inheritance. A king made an absolute decree
that certain lands or property belonged to someone. Once the declaration was made, then the lands continued to be passed down to that
person's heirs. That is why this word *mulkana* is chosen, especially
with regard to Abraham and the promise of the land of Canaan for
his inheritance.

Galatians 3:16-18 APNT
Now the promise [mulkana] was promised [melak] to Abraham
and to his seed. And he did not say to him, "To your seeds" as to
many, but TO YOUR SEED as to one, who is the Messiah.
And this I say, that the covenant, which was previously established
by God in Christ, the law, which was four hundred and thirty years
after, is not able to set it aside and make the promise [mulkana]
void.
Now if the inheritance was by the law, then it was not by promise
[mulkana]. But God gave it to Abraham by promise [mulkana].

The *mulkana* to Abraham has three parts. The promise to Abraham
was an absolute declaration that: 1) he would inherit the land, 2)
Christ (the seed) would come from his lineage, and 3) he would be
a father of many nations. The promise was revealed to Abraham
over a period of time beginning in Genesis 15:1. Abraham took the

declared words of God and believed them literally. The promise is further elaborated in Genesis 17.

Genesis 17:4-8 KJV
As for me, behold, my covenant is with thee, and thou shalt be a father of many nations.
Neither shall thy name any more be called Abram, but thy name shall be Abraham; for a father of many nations have I made thee.
And I will make thee exceeding fruitful, and I will make nations of thee, and kings shall come out of thee.
And I will establish my covenant between me and thee and thy seed after thee in their generations for an everlasting covenant, to be a God unto thee, and to thy seed after thee.
And I will give unto thee, and to thy seed after thee, the land wherein thou art a stranger, all the land of Canaan, for an everlasting possession; and I will be their God.

We have seen in the chapter about the Millennial Reign of Christ that this promise will be fulfilled in very specific ways. The Aramaic for the phrase, "father of many nations," is "father to a multitude of the Gentiles" in Romans 4:17. This three-fold promise of the land as an inheritance, the seed of Christ, and the father of many nations was a *mulkana* to Abraham. It was not earned; it was an arbitrary declaration made by God to him. God will bring to pass his declaration.

There are two passages where the two different Aramaic words for promise occur together. These now become clearer when the different emphases of the words are understood. The two passages are Galatians 3:14-29 and Hebrews 6:12-17. The whole context of Galatians 3 is that the law did not annul the promise made to Abraham. This promise, as we have seen, included the land, blessings upon the nations, and that the seed would come from him. All of the uses are *mulkana* except in two verses, 14 and 19.

Galatians 3:14, 18-19 APNT
that the blessing of Abraham might be on the Gentiles by Jesus
Christ and [that] we would receive the promise [shudaya] of the
Spirit through faith.
Now if the inheritance was by the law, then it was not by promise
[mulkana]. But God gave it to Abraham by promise [mulkana].
Why then [was] the law? It was added because of transgression
until that seed should come to whom was the promise [shudaya].
And the law was given by way of angels, by the hand of a media-
tor.

Shudaya is used when it is talking about the Holy Spirit because the
gift is the outward witness or manifested fulfillment of the promise.
The gift of Holy Spirit was dependent on the fulfillment of the promise of the seed, Christ. All of the rest of the discussion has to do with
the law not negating the promise of the land and blessings to Abraham, which was a *mulkana*, an arbitrary declaration of God. The
whole *mulkana* will be completely fulfilled during the Millennial
Reign of Christ when all the land described in Genesis will belong
to Abraham and his descendants.

Hebrews 6:12-17 discusses the promise to Abraham and how God
confirmed it with an oath. In verse 17 the two words for promise are
used together.

Hebrews 6:17 APNT
Because of this, God especially wanted to show to the heirs of the
promise [mulkana] that his promise [shudaya] would not change,
so he bound it with oaths.

Murdock translates the last phrase with *shudaya*: "that his promising
was irreversible." God personally guaranteed the promise and it will
be completely fulfilled.

All the declarations of God are faithful and can be relied upon. They are absolute declarations from someone who is able to bring them to pass. We have been given the fulfillment of part of the promise to Abraham, because we have Holy Spirit and are partakers of the divine nature from the seed, Christ. Holy Spirit is the manifested witness and fulfillment (*shudaya*) of the promise. We are also heirs of the rest of the promise (*mulkana*) to Abraham. That includes the declaration that the land will be ours and the blessings to the nations.

Someone once counted over nine hundred promises in the Bible. God is faithful to keep each and every one, for if he declared it (just like a king), it will come to pass. Which ones do you need to see fulfilled in your life?

Acts 2:39 APNT
For the promise [shudaya] is to you and to your children and to
all those who are far away, those whom God will call.

This book has been the summary of the "hope of his calling." And as I mentioned in the first chapter, it is something that we need to be able to replay in our minds like a movie and to know beyond a shadow of a doubt.

Ephesians 1:18-21 APNT
and [that] the eyes of your hearts would be enlightened, so that
you would know what is the hope of his calling and what is the
wealth of the glory of his inheritance in the holy [ones]
and what is the abundance of the greatness of his power in us, in
those who believe, according to the working of the might of his
power.
[This is] he who worked in Christ and raised him from the dead
and seated him at his right hand in heaven,

higher than all rulers and authorities and powers and lordships and higher than every name that is named, not only in this world, but in the coming [one] also.

His calling to us in the body of Christ means we will enjoy all the benefits Christ does. We are fellowheirs with him and we share fully in everything that he has and will have. That includes new spiritual bodies, complete redemption and a full inheritance as sons of God. Christ is higher than all rulers and authorities in the coming age also. We will be with him as one from the time of the gathering together until the new heavens and earth are established and then into eternity (as far as we can see and beyond).

Romans 8:15-18 APNT
For you have not received the spirit of bondage again to fear, but you have received the Spirit of adoption by which we call, "Father, our Father."
And the Spirit gives testimony to our spirit that we are the sons of God.
And if [we are] sons, [then] also heirs, heirs of God and fellow-heirs of Jesus Christ, that if we suffer with him, we will also be glorified with him.
For I consider that the sufferings of this time are not equal to the glory that will be revealed in us.

If we are suffering with him now in this time, it is nothing compared to the glorious time when we will be with him forever. We have the gift of the Spirit now so that we may be assured of what will come in the future. That is why it is called the "hope" of his calling. We can look expectantly to what is to come and hold fast to the confidence that brings, knowing God will bring to pass his promises in EVERY WAY. What joy to know that we can wait with courage and steadfastness for the hope to unfold exactly as God said it would.

The Phillips translation of Romans 8 is fantastic. Even the whole creation is waiting for the "rescue."

Romans 8:19-21 Phillips
The whole creation is on tiptoe to see the wonderful sight of the sons of God coming into their own. The world of creation cannot as yet see reality, not because it chooses to be blind, but because in God's purpose it has been so limited– yet it has been given hope. And the hope is that in the end the whole of created life will be rescued from the tyranny of change and decay, and have its share in that magnificent liberty which can only belong to the children of God!

We CAN have patience and "settle down" to wait for the full manifestation of the hope of the "coming of the Son of Man."

Romans 8:22-25 Phillips
It is plain to anyone with eyes to see that at the present time all created life groans in a sort of universal travail. And it is plain, too, that we who have a foretaste of the Spirit are in a state of painful tension, while we wait for that redemption of our bodies which will mean that at last we have realised our full sonship in him. We were saved by this hope, but in our moments of impatience let us remember that hope always means waiting for something that we haven't yet got. But if we hope for something we cannot see, then we must settle down to wait for it in patience.

"The whole creation is on tiptoe to see the wonderful sight of the sons of God coming into their own."

THE HOPE OF HIS CALLING

COMFORT OF THE SCRIPTURES

All of the events that we have covered have been portrayed in such a fashion so that we can have patience and hope, and also great comfort.

Romans 15:4 APNT
For everything that was previously written is for our instruction. It was written so that by the patience and by the comfort of the scriptures we would have hope.

Comfort means to console, encourage or exhort. In 1 Thessalonians 4:18, it says that when someone dies to "comfort one another with these words," that is, the truths regarding the gathering together and the coming kingdom. God is the God of all comfort and he comforts us during our trials and will continue to comfort everyone through to the *telos* end.

2 Corinthians 1:3-4 APNT
Blessed be God, the Father of our Lord Jesus Christ, the Father of mercies and the God of all comfort,
he who comforts us in all our pressures, so that we would also be able to comfort those who are in all pressures with that comfort [with] which we are comforted by God.

This hope of the coming of our Lord and the coming of the Son of Man is what generates great strength to deal with every kind of pressure, including death. Down through the ages, many Old Testament believers—Noah, Abraham, David, Jehoshaphat, and Hezekiah, and also many New Testament believers, including Paul, Barnabas, Timothy and Peter—all relied on this hope to continue to stand against the adversity in their lives.

THE HOPE OF HIS CALLING

2 Corinthians 1:8-11 APNT
Now we want you to know, our brothers, about the pressure that
we had in Asia. We were greatly pressured beyond our strength, to
the point that our lives were about to end.
And we resigned ourselves to death, that we should not have confi-
dence in ourselves, but in God who raises the dead [and it was]
he who rescued us from violent deaths. And we trust that he will
rescue us again
with the aid of your prayer for us, that his gift toward us may be a
blessing that is done on behalf of many and many will give thanks
to him for us.

God has rescued us and will rescue us again! Like Abraham, we are
looking for a city whose designer and builder is God.

Hebrews 11:8-10 ESV
By faith Abraham obeyed when he was called to go out to a place
that he was to receive as an inheritance. And he went out, not
knowing where he was going.
By faith he went to live in the land of promise, as in a foreign land,
living in tents with Isaac and Jacob, heirs with him of the same
promise.
For he was looking forward to the city that has foundations, whose
designer and builder is God.

Therefore, my exhortation to you is to comfort one another with
these words and to encourage one another until the day of our Lord
Jesus Christ.

2 Thessalonians 2:16-17 APNT
Now our Lord Jesus Christ and God our Father, who loved us and
gave us everlasting comfort and good hope by his grace,
comfort your hearts and establish [you] in every word and in every
good work.

CHART OF THE SEQUENCE OF EVENTS

Sequence	Events	Scriptures
The Gathering Together	Coming of our Lord Dead in Christ rise first Those alive in Christ are changed Meeting of our Lord in the air	1 Thessalonians 4:13-18
	The last trump	1 Corinthians 15:51-57
	Judgment seat (bema)	2 Corinthians 5:10 1 Corinthians 3:11-15
	The great mystery complete	Ephesians 3:8-9
	Day of Christ	Philippians 1:10; 2:16
	Day of our Lord Jesus Christ	1 Corinthians 1:8; 5:5 2 Corinthians 1:14
	Day of Redemption	Ephesians 4:30
The Beginning of Sorrows	False messiahs, propaganda campaign Wars and rumors of wars Famine Death from earthquakes, pestilence, natural disasters and wild beasts	Matthew 24:4-8 Mark 13:5-8 Luke 21:8-11a
	1st four seals ¼ of the population of the earth is killed	Revelation 6:1-8
	One generation	Luke 21:29-33
The Rise of the Antichrist	"Man of sin"	2 Thessalonians 2:3
	"Little horn"	Daniel 7:7-8
	Rise of powerful "king"	Daniel 7:23-26 Daniel 8:23-25
	"Vile person"	Daniel 11:21-44
	"Beast"	Revelation 13:1-18
	Makes covenant with Israel for seven years Temple rebuilt and offerings reinstated	Daniel 9:24-27
	Reign of "harlot"	Revelation 17:1-7 Revelation 17:14-18
	False death and resurrection	Revelation 17:8-13

CHART OF THE SEQUENCE OF EVENTS

The Abomination of Desolation	Gospel is preached throughout the age	Matthew 24:14 Mark 13:9-13 Luke 21:12-19
	Two witnesses	Revelation 11:4-12 Zechariah 4:12-14
	Abomination of desolation set up in middle of 7th week	Daniel 8:9-14 Daniel 9:27; 11:31; 12:11
	Antichrist displays himself as God	2 Thessalonians 2:3-5
	Great tribulation begins	Matthew 24:15-26 Mark 13:14-20 Luke 21:20-21
	Strong delusion	2 Thessalonians 2:8-12
The Great Tribulation	Mark of the beast	Revelation 13:17-18
	5th seal	Revelation 6:9-11 Luke 19:43-44
	1,260 days or 42 months	Revelation 11:2-3
	Day of Jacob's trouble	Jeremiah 30:7 Daniel 12:11 Habakkuk 3:16
	Day of their calamity	Obadiah 1:13-14
	Day of visitation	Isaiah 10:3-7
	Indignation	Isaiah 10:24-27 Daniel 11:36
The Beginning of the Day of the Lord	Great signs Sun and moon darkened, stars fall Powers of heaven are shaken Moon turned to blood	Matthew 24:29 Mark 13:24-25 Luke 21:25-26 Joel 2:10-11, 31 Isaiah 13:9-13 Ezekiel 32:7-8 Acts 2:19-20
	6th seal Earthquake	Revelation 6:12-16
	144,000 sealed	Revelation 7:1-8
	The day of the Lord begins	Acts 2:20
The Vengeance and wrath of God	Day of wrath	Romans 1:18 Isaiah 13:9 Zephaniah 1:14-15 Joel 2:1-3 Amos 5:18-19
	Day of vengeance	Luke 21:22-24 Isaiah 61:2
	7th seal	Revelation 8:7-9:19 Revelation 16:1-17:21
	Babylon is destroyed	Revelation 18

The Day of God Almighty	Kings of the East	Revelation 16:12
		Isaiah 49:12
	From north country	Jeremiah 46:10; 50:9
		Jeremiah 51:27-58
	Antichrist and his troops	Daniel 11:45
		Zechariah 12-14
	Coalition of Gog and Magog	Ezekiel 38-39
The Coming of the Son of Man	Banner of the Son of Man seen in the clouds	Matthew 24:27-30
		Revelation 1:7
	Coming of Christ on white horse as King of kings	Revelation 19:11-16
		Jude 14
	The harvest of the earth	Revelation 14:14-16
	Carrion birds invited to the "great supper of God," wine-press of wrath	Revelation 19:17-18
		Revelation 14:18-20
		Ezekiel 39:17-22
	Defeat of Antichrist's army at Jerusalem	Zechariah 14:12-15
	Beast and false prophet cast into the lake of fire	Revelation 19:19-21
The Kingdom Established	Jesus' feet land on Mount of Olives and mountain splits in two	Zechariah 14:4
	Gathering of the elect	Matthew 24:31
		Mark 13:27-37
		Luke 17:25-36
		Deuteronomy 30:3-5
		Ezekiel 34:12-13
		Isaiah 27:12-13
	144,000 with Christ on Mount Zion	Revelation 14:1-5
	Satan is bound	Revelation 20:1-3
	Judgment of the Gentiles	Joel 3:1-2, 14
		Matthew 25:31-46
	Resurrection of the Just	Revelation 20:4
		Isaiah 26:19
		Ezekiel 37:1-14
		Joel 2:28-29
	Marriage Supper of the Lamb	Revelation 19:7
		John 14:1-3
		Revelation 21:9-12

The Millennial Reign of Christ	Changes in the Land	Daniel 2:44-45 Micah 4:1-7 Jeremiah 3:17 Isaiah 35:5-10 Isaiah 65:19-25 Ezekiel 39:8-16 Zechariah 14:16-19 Psalm 2:8-9
	Holy Oblation and the New Temple	Ezekiel 40-48 Isaiah 56:7 Isaiah 4:2-6
The Telos	Satan loosed and deceives the nations	Revelation 20:7-8
	Fire from God consumes the enemies	Revelation 20:9
	Devil cast into the lake of fire	Revelation 20:10 Ezekiel 28:17-19
	Resurrection of the unjust Great white throne judgment	Revelation 20:11-13 2 Peter 2:9
	Death and grave and all judged as wicked cast in lake of fire	Revelation 20:14-15 1 Corinthians 15:24-28
	Heavens and earth dissolved, the end of the day of the Lord	2 Peter 3:10-12
	New heavens and earth	2 Peter 3:13 Revelation 21:1-5 Isaiah 65:17

BIBLIOGRAPHY

Anderson, Sir Robert. *The Coming Prince.* Grand Rapids, Michigan: Kregel Publications, 1984.

Barker, Kenneth, et al. *The NIV Study Bible.* Grand Rapids, Michigan: Zondervan Publishing House, 1995.

Barnes, Albert. *Notes on the Bible,* E-sword.

Benner, Jeff A. *The Ancient Hebrew Lexicon of the Bible.* College Station, Texas: Virtualbookworm.com Publishing, 2005.

Bromiley, Geoffrey, ed. *Theological Dictionary of the Old Testament (Kittel), Abridged in One Volume.* Grand Rapids, Michigan: William B. Eerdmans Publishing Company, 1985.

Brown, Francis, S.R. Driver, Charles A. Briggs, eds. *The New Brown-Driver-Briggs-Gesenius Hebrew and English Lexicon.* Christian Copyrights, Inc., 1983.

Brown, Raymond E., Joseph A. Fitzmyer, Roland E. Murphy. *The Jerome Biblical Commentary.* Englewood Cliffs, New Jersey: Prentice-Hall, Inc., 1968.

Bullinger, E.W. *A Critical Lexicon and Concordance to the English and Greek New Testament.* Grand Rapids, Michigan: Zondervan Publishing House, 1975.

Bullinger, E.W. *Commentary on Revelation.* Grand Rapids, Michigan: Kregel Publications, 1984.

Bullinger, E.W. *Figures of Speech Used in the Bible.* Grand Rapids, Michigan: Baker Book House, 1968.

Byrd, J. Mike. *The Millennial Kingdom and the Final Judgments Revisited.* 2018.

Campbell, Gordon. *Reading Revelation A Thematic Approach.* Cambridge: James Clarke and Co., 2012.

BIBLIOGRAPHY

Capps, Charles. *End-Time Events, Journey to the End of the Age*. Tulsa, Oklahoma: Harrison House, 1997.

Chafer, Lewis. *Satan His Motives and Methods*. Grand Rapids, Michigan: Zondervan Publishing House, 1971.

Clarke, Adam. *The New Testament of our Lord and Saviour Jesus Christ, Commentary on the Bible*. New York: Abingdon Press. Volumes 1-6.

Constable, Thomas L. *Notes on Revelation*, www.studylight.org.

Cummins, Walter, *The Acceptable Year of the Lord*. Franklin, Ohio: Scripture Consulting, 2005.

Douglas, J. D., ed. *New Bible Dictionary*. Wheaton, Illinois: Tyndale House Publishers, 1987.

Fuchtenbaum, Arnold. *The Footsteps of the Messiah*. Tustin, California: Ariel Ministries Press, 1982.

Girdlestone, Robert Baker. *Synonyms of the Old Testament*. Grand Rapids, Michigan: Wm. B. Eerdmans Publishing Company, 1897.

Harper, Larry D. *The Antichrist*. Mesquite, Texas: The Elijah Project, 2003.

Harris, R. Laird, Gleason L. Archer, Jr., Bruce K. Waltke, eds. *Theological Wordbook of the Old Testament* 2 volumes. Chicago, Illinois: Moody Press, 1980.

Hendriksen, William. *More Than Conquerors*. Grand Rapids, Michigan: BakerBooks, 2015.

Hixson, J. B. and Mark Fontecchio. *What Lies Ahead*. Brenham, Texas: Lucid Books, 2013.

Jamieson, Robert, A. R. Fausset, David Brown. *Commentary on the Whole Bible*. Grand Rapids, Michigan: Zondervan Publishing House, 1962.

BIBLIOGRAPHY

Jennings, William. *Lexicon to the Syriac New Testament.* London: Oxford University Press, 1926.

Jeremiah, Dr. David. *Agents of the Apocalypse.* Carol Stream, Illinois: Tyndale House Publishers, 2014.

Johnson, Ken. *The End-Times by the Ancient Church Fathers,* 2016.

Josephus, Flavius. *Wars of the Jews.* www.biblestudytools.com

Kostenberger, Andreas J. Alexander E. Stewart and Apollo Makara. *Jesus and the Future.* Wooster, Ohio: Weaver Book Company, 2017.

LaHaye, Tim, Thomas Ice. *Charting the End Times.* Eugene, Oregon: Harvest House Publishers, 2001.

Larkin, Clarence. *The Book of Revelation.* Philadelphia, Pennsylvania: Rev. Clarence Larkin Estate, 1919.

Lasseigne, Jeff. *Unlocking the Last Days.* Grand Rapids, Michigan: BakerBooks, 2011.

Lightfoot, John. *A Commentary on the New Testament from the Talmud and Hebraica. 4 vols.* Peabody, Massachusetts: Hendrickson Publishers, 1989.

Martin, Ernest. *The Life and Times of the Antichrist.* Portland, Oregon: Associates for Scriptural Knowledge, 1992.

Murdock, James. *The New Testament.* New York: Stanford and Swords, 1852.

Nave, Orville J. *The New Nave's Topical Bible.* Grand Rapids, Michigan: Zondervan Publishing House, 1969.

Orr, James, ed, *The International Standard Bible Encyclopedia.* www.biblestudytools.com

Palmer, Earl F. *The Preacher's Commentary, 1, 2 & 3 John/Revelation.* Nashville, Tennessee: Thomas Nelson Publishers, 1982.

BIBLIOGRAPHY

Parks, Jerry L. *The Millennium Handbook,* CreateSpace Publishing, 2018.

Pentecost, Dwight J. *Things to Come.* Grand Rapids, Michigan: Zondervan Publishing House, 1964.

Pentecost, Dwight J. *Thy Kingdom Come.* Scripture Press Publications, 1990.

Prideaux, Humphrey. *The Old and New Testament Connected in the History of the Jews.* Oxford at the University Press, 1861.

Rand, Howard B. *Study in Daniel.* Haverhill, Massachusetts: Destiny Publishers, 1963.

Rand, Howard B. *Study in Revelation.* Haverhill, Massachusetts: Destiny Publishers, 1947.

Rhodes, Ron. *The End Times in Chronological Order.* Eugene, Oregon: Harvest House Publishers, 2012.

Rice, Edwin W. *People's Dictionary of the Bible.* Philadelphia, Pennsylvania: American Sunday-School Union, 1904.

Richards, Lawrence O. *New International Encyclopedia of Bible Words.* Grand Rapids, Michigan: Zondervan Publishing House, 1991.

Richardson, Alan, ed. *A Theological Word Book of the Bible.* New York: Macmillan Publishing Company, 1950.

Ritchie, J. M. *Messiah the Prince.* New York: Exposition Press, 1952.

Ryken, Leland, ed. *Dictionary of Biblical Imagery.* Downers Grove, Illinois: InterVarsity Press, 1998.

Schmitt, John W. and J. Carl Laney. *Messiah's Coming Temple.* Grand Rapids, Michigan: Kregel Publications, 1997.

Schneider, Rabbi Kurt. *The Book of Revelation Decoded.* Lake Mary, Florida: Charisma House, 2017.

Seiss, Joseph. *The Apocalypse.* Grand Rapids, Michigan: Kregel

BIBLIOGRAPHY

Publications, 1987.

Smith, J. Payne. *A Compendious Syriac Dictionary*. London: Oxford at the Clarendon Press, 1967.

Smith, Jerome H. *The New Treasury of Scripture Knowledge*. Google Books, 1992.

Smith, William. *A Dictionary of the Bible*. Grand Rapids, Michigan: Zondervan Publishing, 1948.

Stendall, Russell M. *The Seventh Trumpet and the Seven Thunders*. Aneko Press, 2013.

Thayer, Joseph Henry. *The New Thayer's Greek-English Lexicon*. Christian Copyrights, Inc., 1981.

Vine, W.E. *Vine's Expository Dictionary of Old and New Testament Words*. Old Tappan, New Jersey: Fleming H. Revell Company, 1981.

Walvoord, John. *Daniel*. Chicago: Moody Publishers, 2012.

Walvoord, John. *The Millennial Kingdom*. Grand Rapids, Michigan: Zondervan Publishing, 1959.

Walvoord, John. *The Revelation of Jesus Christ*. Chicago: Moody Press, 1966.

Webster, Noah. *Noah Webster's First Edition of an American Dictionary of the English Language*. San Francisco: Foundation for American Christian Education, 1967.

Wiersbe, Warren W. *Key Words of the Christian Life*. Grand Rapids, Michigan: Baker Book House, 2002.

ABOUT THE AUTHOR

Janet Magiera is an ordained minister and the founder of Light of the Word Ministry, a ministry dedicated to teaching and making known the understanding of the Aramaic language, figures of speech and customs of the Bible. In 1979, under the tutelage of a student of Dr. George M. Lamsa, Jan began pursuing a course of study of the Aramaic Peshitta New Testament. For over 40 years, she has taught in Bible fellowships and churches in the United States and other countries, using insight from her understanding of the Biblical languages. Many articles and teachings of interest are available on the Light of the Word Ministry website, www.lightofword.org.

In 1990, Jan began compiling a database of the Aramaic Peshitta New Testament. As computer technology increased over the years, she expanded and developed the database to generate a series of research tools to study the New Testament. The entire database originally was developed as a software module in BibleWorks and is now also available online at www.aramaicdb.lightofword.org. The *Aramaic Peshitta New Testament Translation* was the first book published in 2006 of a complete *Aramaic Peshitta New Testament Library*. The library includes an interlinear, lexicon, concordance, and parallel translations. There is an app of the Aramaic translation on both ITunes and GooglePlay, as well as various electronic versions of her books and the translations.

Jan has also authored several topical books on Biblical subjects, *Enriched in Everything* on giving, *Members in Particular* on the Body of Christ, and *The Armor of Victory* on the armor of God. She also has published a book on Hebrew and Aramaic word pictures called *The Fence of Salvation*.

She and her husband Glen currently live in San Diego, California. Together they have four children and eleven grandchildren.